The Students Practice Work Book

PRACTICAL COMPUTER EDUCATION

CONI T. TAWONG

TOBBY VISION

The Students Practice Work Book
Practical Computer Education Vol. I
First Edition 2015
© 2015, Cornelius Tfurndabi Tawong.
Bamenda-Cameroon.

Cover design
Tobby Vision Computers Ltd
Email: corneliustawong@yahoo.com
tobbyvision@yahoo.com
P. O. Box 309 Bamenda

DEDICATION

The Students Practice Work Book Is Dedicated To:

My late grandfather

NGWANG   KUMANTA   MUNKI
&
CAROL   HISHON
Each of them now peacefully resting with the Lord.

Recommendations to Teachers
Tests and Examinations: Written, Practical and Oral
By Dr. Vunan Vugar Paul (Ph.D Education)

Introduction

Testing is a generic term. "Testing" refers to any kind of school activity which results in a mark or comment being entered in a record book, or on a sheet, checklist or anecdotal list. In other words, observation, the writing of an essay, a short quiz, a classroom test or a cross–grade examination can all be referred to as "testing". On the other hand, the term "test" is used to denote the structured, formal, practical and oral or written evaluation of student achievement.

The word "test" is frequently used to denote both tests and examinations. Examinations are tests which are school scheduled, rather than classroom scheduled. Traditionally, they have tended to cover more of the curriculum and be assigned a greater percentage of the student's mark than any individual classroom test or assignment. Diagnosis is not a major focus; rather, the main emphasis is upon written, practical and oral tests, the outcome of which is recorded as part of a term or a year's mark.

For the most part, tests and examinations are not appropriate in the Primary Division.

Planning Evaluation

In planning a course of study or classroom program, teachers should clearly indicate, at the outset, the evaluation component and, as soon as possible, make it known to students. Testing is an integral part of the teaching–learning process and therefore should receive as much emphasis in planning as the other course components. In order that teachers may plan their program, they should decide in advance when they are going to give a pre–test to find out what the students know and do not know. Pre-testing will often save valuable classroom time, because if the class or group already has adequate knowledge or skill, the teacher may proceed to a new topic or activity.

Sometimes, tests are constructed on the spur of the moment under the pressure of time. Testing, however, is so important that a re-allocation of scarce teacher time is necessary to ensure that planning for evaluation takes place. An important aspect of this planning is establishing the necessary balance and integration of the testing component with the rest of the curriculum.

Balance and Integration

Balance

A good program neither has too many tests so that it becomes a testing program rather than a learning situation, nor should it have so few tests that students and teachers have no consistent indication of progress.

Another aspect of balance is the consideration of the amount of classroom time to be devoted to formal testing. In a set period of classroom time, teachers should decide what proportion of the time should be devoted to testing. This will probably vary considerably; for example, some aspects of a subject may require only ten minutes in a predetermined number of days for adequate testing, while other aspects may require longer periods of time and longer intervals between the tests.

Integration

Tests should be an integral part of the teaching–learning process and should not be separated from the on–going daily classroom teaching and laboratory practicals. For most of the time in the classroom, the student's mind–set is feeling of rapport with peers and teacher. In an unstructured testing program, the mind–set can shift so that the student sees the teacher as an adversary, rather than as a partner in the learning process. This change of role reinforces the lack of integration between learning and testing.

The student should see testing as part of the learning process, and, as much as possible, not be threatened by it. One way to achieve this necessary atmosphere is to ensure that there is a constant, powerful connection among teaching–learning objectives, classroom and laboratory activities, and testing activities. When testing is perceived as a learning process, the students have an opportunity to display what they have learned, and identify topics for further study or investigation. When testing is viewed in this way by teacher and student, then testing is no longer a process of merely acquiring a mark for a report card.

A fully integrated teaching–testing component of a program should provide test situations only when there is a logical and obvious completion of a theme, section or unit of study. It becomes almost impossible, therefore, to follow the above practice and also require that every Thursday afternoon there will be a test. Some aspects of subjects, however, such as Computer Studies lend itself to a fixed pattern. For example, in studying the Microsoft Windows environment, a class may be pre–tested on Monday, study from Tuesday and Thursday, and be given a post–test on Friday. This pattern is based on logical units of study.

88 Key Questions to ask about Tests and Examinations

88 questions about tests and examinations may, at first glance, seem outrageous. However, there is no intention that every question must be considered each time a testing program is planned and each time a test is prepared and marked. Nevertheless, the questions raise issues which are fundamental to all aspects of the testing program. At various points in the testing program process, teachers should consider the issues raised by these questions.

Questions to ask oneself when planning the year's Test

- In my school's calendar, are there specific times set aside for formal tests or examinations? - If so, what are they?
- How can I plan the rest of my evaluation program around these dates?
- At what points in my program should there be a test?
- How many tests will this plan produce?
- Are there too many, just enough, or too few tests?
- If there are too many tests, which units can I combine for testing purposes?
- If there are too few, where are the logical points within a unit where I may test?
- Have I considered my schedule of tests in the context of the student's total school program?
- Will this schedule be fair to the students or will they be over–burdened?
- How can I provide variety in my proposed evaluation program?

- Have I made provision for a number of different evaluation procedures other than tests, such as observation, oral and practicals?
- Within my test schedule, have I made provision for a variety of test techniques, such as objective–style questions, essay–style questions, sight passages, and open–book tests?
- Have I provided adequate time for marking the tests of my students?
- Will this time permit me to give personal attention to each of my student's tests?
- What proportion of marks for reporting purposes will be based on tests? What proportion will be based on other evaluation components such as observation, practicals and participation?
- Is this proportion fair and equitable for the particular students I am teaching?
- Is there a school policy regarding missed tests? If not, do I have a policy?
- Is my evaluation program integrated with the objectives of my course or program?
- What possible modifications for testing and the testing schedule must I make for students with exceptionalities?

Questions to ask oneself before building a particular Test

- Why am I giving this test?
- What do I now know, and what do I hope to learn from this test, about each of my students, the class and the curriculum?
- What do I want my students to learn from this test?
- What is the most appropriate type of test to find out this information?
- How is test related to the course objectives? Which of the course or unit objectives will be measured in this test?
- How much weight should I give to each objective that I wish to measure?
- Which questions will I relate to which objectives?
- Have I prepared my students for the method of evaluation and styles of questions I am proposing to use?

- Do my students have a clear understanding of my evaluation techniques and marking procedures?
- Will the amount of time I have provided for each question be sufficient? Is the total time allotted for the test sufficient so that the students have adequate time to answer the questions, re-read their work and revise where necessary?
- Is the proportion of marks for each question congruent to the difficulty of the question and amount of time needed to answer it?
- Will the distributions of the difficulty of the questions take into account the varying levels of ability within the class?
- In my marking scheme for each question, what will be considered a reasonable and acceptable answer?
- What are my expectations regarding overall student performance on this test?
- Have I allocated time for follow-up activities after I have marked the test?
- In constructing and marking this test, have I made provisions for any students with exceptionalities?
- Are the questions clear and concise?
- Am I asking for too much information in the time available?
- Have the questions been asked using vocabulary the students will understand?
- Is there a suitable distribution of difficult and less difficult questions?
- Did I try out the questions on an informed colleague, if possible?
- Will the students have to supply too much information to answer the question in the time available?
- Have I been able to work through and answer the questions in a third to half the time given the students?
- Is the amount of time required to answer the test question commensurate with the amount of time required to read the material, for example, in a sight passage?
- If there are choices or alternate questions, are they of equal difficulty and worth?

- Are the instructions for guiding students' choices among questions or sections clearly stated?
- Have I considered the effect on the students of the format and general appearance (for example, legibility) of the test?
- Have I asked questions which require higher practice experience as well as factual recall?
- Have I prepared a detailed marking scheme for the whole test?
- Does the test indicate the mark distribution and suggested time allocation for answering?
- Have I checked to see whether other tests for the same students have been scheduled for the same day?
- Have I tried to avoid inappropriate times during the week for the test?
- Have the students been given sufficient advance notice in order to prepare adequately for the test?
- Have the students been informed about: The date of the test; what is to be covered by the test; the length of the test; Kinds of questions to be used (for example objective style, MCQs or open–book)?
- Have the students been taught how to answer the type of question to be used on the test? (The test experience should never be the first experience for any type of question).
- Have the students been taught how to study for a particular type of question?
- Have students been taught how to deal with key directing words in questions such as "compare", "identify", "state the importance of"?
- Have I ensured that the students know the meaning of all the words I have used in asking the questions?
- Have I considered appropriate modifications for students with exceptionalities?
- Have I allowed for time for students to ask me questions for clarification during the day or so leading up to the test?
- Have I informed the students of the materials, instruments or storage devices that they will need to bring with them to the test? Are the students aware of the routines which will likely follow if they fail to bring the appropriate materials to the test?

- Have I ensured that all the material I need for conducting the test is present in the classroom?
- Have I made sure that the room in which the test is to be given is suitable?
- Were the questions or problems clearly stated?
- Is there evidence that a number of students, including the exceptional students, had inadequate time to complete satisfactorily particular questions or the whole test?
- Is there evidence that a number of students were ill–prepared to answer a particular question?
- Was the lack of preparation the result of inadequate study on the part of the students?
- Was the material which was taught too abstract for the intellectual development of the students?
- Was the method of presentation of the material in class clear and sufficiently extensive?
- Was the method of presentation of the material in class appropriate for the level of student ability?
- Was there sufficient time devoted to follow–up activities after presentation of the material in class and prior to the test?
- Did I construct the questions appropriate to the specific level of ability of the students?
- Is there evidence that I must adjust my marking scheme and re–score tests already marked?
- Am I constantly on the look–out for unexpected, acceptable responses which differ from those listed in the marking scheme?
- If the number of students obtaining a low mark or a high mark is above expectations, how am I going to use the marks?
- If the level of achievement on the test was very low, what changes should I make in my methods of classroom presentation and follow–up?
- If the results of other teachers' classes using the same test differ greatly from mine, what could be the cause of this discrepancy?
- What other methods of evaluation might have been more useful?

- Did the test results reflect adequately the provisions that I made for students with exceptionalities when I prepared the test?
- Were the questions on the test which required higher level thinking too easy, adequate or too difficult?
- Should I use this test again?

Now what do I do?

Once you have assessed the results and suitability of the test, some of the following suggested activities could be carried out, where deemed necessary?

- Identify any students who may require re–teaching, further study or assistance, and re–testing.
- Provide opportunities for individual student–teacher conferences for joint evaluation and planning.
- Encourage students, from time to time, to write to reaction paper regarding their perceptions of the test;
- Re–test with a more appropriate instrument or method;
- Teach or review appropriate instrument or method;
- Teach or review appropriate study techniques;
- Review or re–teach the necessary part or section using a different method of presentation as required;

No Surprises!

It is important that, whenever teachers are using tests and examinations, they should make sure that all students have had experience with all types of questions to be used.

Furthermore, if a teacher occasionally wishes to use a "surprise test" to find out what the students do or do not know, the practice can be beneficial for both students and teacher. However, this form of surprise test should be seen as diagnostic because it tells the teacher and students what is or is not known at that time without preparation.

Therefore, any comment, grade or mark assigned to such a test should not be used in calculating the term or final mark for reporting purposes. The students also should be assured that this is an information–gathering exercise and not a formal evaluation. A surprise test must never be punitive nor be given to obtain an immediate mark to meet a reporting deadline.

Another form of 'surprise test" and one which must be avoided, occurs when an evaluation has been announced for a particular time, but then is re–scheduled at the last minute to a later date. Therefore, unless there are unavoidable circumstances which students understand, tests and examinations must occur as scheduled.

Instructions to Students

Tests and examinations are an essential part of learning. The Students Practice Work Book is conceived to facilitate student understanding and assimilation of material. As such students are advised to consider this Practise Work Book as a progress chart. For it to be of any use, the student must endeavour to answer all the questions of each chapter. Do not go to the next chapter if you have not answered all the questions on the previous Chapter.

This Work Book is designed to accompany the main textbook **Practical Computer Education Vol. I**. Students are advised to work hand-in-hand with their instructors because getting to the right answers will entail doing actual practical work and with the help of the main textbook Practical Computer Education.

Chapter One: Introduction to Computers

1. What is a computer?...
   ....
   ....(4mks)

2. What do you understand by data?...
   ....(1mk)

3. What is information?..
   ....(1mk)

4. Differentiate between data and information..................................
   ....
   ....(2mks)

5. Name the four basic operations that a computer must be able to
   perform (i)...(ii)...................................
   (iii)...(iv)...................................(2mks)

6. A computer is not a single device. It is made up of several devices
   that function together as a system. Give ten examples of such
   devices that make up a computer? (i)........................(ii)..................
   (iii)..........................(iv) ....(v) ....
   (vi) ....(vii) ....(viii) ....
   (ix) ....(x) ....(5mks)

7. Identify two reasons why people study microcomputers (i)..............
   ....(ii).....................................
   ....(2mks)

8. A better way of understanding how the computer functions is to
   know what goes into the computer which is called..................and
   what comes out of the computer which is called...................(2mks)

9. What is an input device?...(1mk)

10. Name four input devices and their uses (i)name...........................
    Use...(ii)name...........................
    Use...(iii)name...........................
    Use...(iv)name...........................
    Use..(4mks)

11. The "thinking" in computers is done by a component known as the
    ....and its performance which is measured in terms
    of the speed with which it executes its operations is called the clock
    frequency and is measured in...................................(2mks).

12. If a processor is not sufficiently cooled, it may develop functional problems or it can stop working. Name devices that are commonly used for reducing the temperature of the processor..........................
....(2mks)

13. The central processing unit (CPU) consists of five sections. Name them (i)........................(ii) ....(iii) ....
(iv) ....(v) .... (5mks)

14. ....refers to the computer's starting up process when the configuration files are loaded into the computer memory   (1mk).

15. What are storage devices?..
Name 4 examples of your choice (i).....................(ii) ....
(iii)...................................(iv) ....(3mks)

16. Write in full the following:
    i) BIOS..
    ii) ROM..
    iii) RAM..(3mks)

17. Storage capacity is measured in bytes, kilobytes (KB), megabytes (MB), gigabytes (GB), terabytes (TB), petabytes (PB) and exabytes (EB). Electricity signals that come from the electricity Company and out of the wall outlet move in a wave motion as shown in the figure (Voltage(v) Vs Time(t) graph). A signal at a maximum level is represented by 1 and a signal at a minimum level by 0 by chips in circuits of a Personal Computer and all digital or electronic equipment function in this manner. A byte of information can be 11000011 or 11111000. 1byte = 8 bits or signals and 1,024 bytes = 1 kilobyte.

a) How many byes make 2kilobytes..

b) ....bytes = 200kilobytes

c) 10,485,760 bytes equals..megabytes

d) 1,073,741,824 bytes equal 1 gigabyte. How many bytes are there in 10 gigabytes (GB)?...

e) The capacity of Luma's mobile telephone memory is 3GB and Dama wants to store his game whose size is 2,147,483,648bytes.

Can Luma's mobile telephone memory be useful for Dama?.............
Explain your answer...
....
....

f)   Which is bigger: Luma's mobile telephone memory of 4GB or Dama's mobile telephone memory of 700KB................................

g)   The demand for high capacity memory drives is on the rise nowadays because many students and their parents are in need of much storage space to store videos, games, pictures etc which are heavy and high capacity files. What capacity of memory in gigabytes would you recommend to your brother for storing his baptism video file of size 20,970,520 bytes....................................

h)   Convert the capacity of the memory you have recommended to your brother into bytes...

i)   Which is bigger 10,000MB or 1Gigabyte?........................(10mks)

18. Which is faster and more reliable – Static RAM OR Dynamic RAM...(1mk)

19. A microcomputer is just one of the types of a computer. Name five other types of computer systems in common usage.......................
....
....
....(5mks)

20. (a) In 1642, the French Mathematician Blaise Pascal invented a machine for performing basic mathematical calculations. The machine was called...............................(b) In 1821, the English Mathematician Charles Babbage invented another machine called..........................to perform mathematical calculations. (c)The names of the three American scientists who jointly developed the first electronic computer known as Electronic Numerical Integrator and Calculator (ENIAC) are...
....
(d) Write in full: (i) PC...
(ii)IBM...
(e)...............................refers to the physical elements of a computer

(f)...also commonly known as programs consist of electronic instructions that tell the hardware how to perform a task.   (6mks)

21. Software can be divided into two groups – System Software and Application Software. Microsoft Windows XP/8/10, Mac, Linux etc are examples of ....software (1mk)

22. ....
....are examples of Application software (2mks)

23. Give one example of a program that falls under the following categories: e.g. Category: Word Processing Example: Microsoft Word

Program	Example
Electronic Spreadsheet	
Database	
Presentation Graphics	
Desktop Publishing	
Web Browsers	

                                                                    (5mks)

24. ....and.. are two ancient computers.   (1mk)

25. ....wrote a brilliant report describing several hardware concepts and that of stored programs for computers.

26. Computer hardware refers to the physical elements of the computer. It is also referred to as the machinery or equipment of the computer. Label the parts of the system unit F, G, H, I, K and L below.

F...G...

H...I..

K...L..

M...

When **M** is Standard English, the pattern is QWERTY. _____ is the pattern when M is French.   (2mks)

Chapter Two: Microsoft Windows Operating System

1) Microsoft Windows 7 uses a graphical user interface (GUI) which appears after you start the computer and contains all the choices available is known as...(1mk)

(b) The desktop contain various icons and a bar at its bottom. This bar is known as..(1mk)

2) The taskbar contains the start button and programs which are open on the computer and the time. You can click the.........................to open the window or the program it represents.   (1mk)

3) ....are pictures that represent programs, folders, files, printer information, computer information and so on in Microsoft Windows Operating System.   (1mk)

4) ....is an onscreen icon that represents your mouse or other selecting device and you use it to select items and choose commands.   (1mk)

5) Your ....and ....identify you to the network server and protect your computer from illegal entry. (1mk)

6) The topmost bar of every program window is known as the title bar. This bar displays the name of the program, file and icon on the left hand side. The right side of the title bar has..............................and ....buttons.   (2mks)

7) Fill in the blank spaces

a) ....are small picture buttons present on the desktop. (1mk)

b) ....bar is found at the bottom of Windows 7 desktop.   (1mk)

c) Clicking the left mouse button twice in quick succession is called................................. (1mk)

d) The .... button is used to reduce the program window into a button (1mk)

e) The Menu bar lies just below the ....in Microsoft Word 2003 (1mk)

f) ....is a place in which deleted files and folders from your harddrive remain until you empty the trash. You can retrieve files, pictures, folders and so on from it after you have deleted them. (1mk)

g) The .... icon on the desktop represent contents of your computer including the hard disc drive, CD drives, DVD drives, applications, folders, files etc (1mk)

8) Click means..(1mk)

9) Double click means...
....(2mks)

10) Right click means..
....(2mks)

11) Shift+click means ....
....(2mks)

12) Ctrl+click means ....
....(2mks)

13) The picture on the right shows the result of using Ctrl+click while resizing a rectangle. You will notice that the result is the same increment on the left and right sides. What would you use Ctrl+click to do on files and folders?..
....(2mks)

14) ....is used for customizing your windows. (1mk)

15) In Microsoft Windows 7 the Start Menu is essentially a ....
....that you can organize and customize to suit your preferences. (1mk)

16) Fill in the blank spaces

i.) A Windows 7 colour scheme that changes the way Windows itself looks and behaves on your screen is called.............................(1mk) ii.) ....is a Windows 7 tool that allows you to quickly view all open windows and programs in either thumbnail or full screen mode.   (1mk)

iii.) ....is a wireless technology for adding devices to your computer.   (1mk)

iv.) The blinking icon on the program window that shows you where the characters you type will appear is called...............or................(1mk)

17) One of the ways you can be working in an application program and entertaining your friend on a PC – a single person use computer with a movie in Windows Media Player is to put the two windows side by side and this is known as....................................(1mk)

18) Explain how you would instantly find anything on your computer using the Windows 7 Start Menu..
....(2mks)

19) Windows 10 is the most recent operating system (system software) developed by Microsoft Corporation. Name ten other operating systems..
....
....
....
....(5mks)

20) Microsoft Word 2014 is an application program and is categorized under Word Processing. Name two other Word Processors you know...(2mks)

21)   The key advantage of Word Processing programs is that they allow users to create a document, check errors of spellings and grammar, change margins, add, delete or reallocate entire paragraphs.

(a)   Name   four   other   categories   of   Application   programs

(i)...............................(ii)...(iii)......
...........................(iv)   ....(2mks)

(b) Name **ONE** program example each under each category above.

(i)...

(ii)...

(iii)...

(iv)..

(c)Name two things which you can create with the programs you have named in (b) (i), (ii), (iii), (iv).

i) Name of program...

Two things you can create with the program.....................................

....

ii) Name of program..

Two things you can create with the program.....................................

....

iii) Name of program...

Two things you can create with the program.....................................

....

iv) Name of program...

Two things you can create with the program.....................................

....(8mks)

22) State all the steps you would use to Start Windows 7.....................

....

....

....(4mks)

23) After the operating system is loaded you will see your desktop which is the background on which icons are found. What are icons?..(1mk)

24) List four icons found on the Windows desktop and their uses

  i.) Icon.....................................use...

 ii.) Icon.....................................use...

iii.) Icon.....................................use...

iv.) Icon.....................................use...

                                                              (4mks)

25) The icon that shows you other computers that are connected to your computer when you double click on it is called.....................

....(1mk)

26) A folder is a place in which you keep your files and a file is a related document which you store with a file name for future reference as we have seen in previous operating systems. In Windows 7, libraries are where you go to manage your documents, music, videos, pictures and other files.

a) Define a Library..
....(2mks)

b) Name the four default libraries in Microsoft Windows 7...................
....
....(2mks)

c) What is the meaning of the word default?..................................
....(2mks)

d) Give also the function of the Windows Clipboard..........................
....(2mks)

27) What will happen if you delete a Library.....................................
....
....(2mks)

28) Files and folders deleted from the computer move to the recycle bin. You can still open the recycle bin and retrieve files and folders and can no longer get them when you have emptied the bin. What happens when you delete a file or folder from within a Library?......
....
....(2mks)

29) Say how you would move gadgets to your windows desktop..........
....
....
....(4mks)

30) In Windows 7 you can easily burn a file to a Compact Disc if you have a CD writer or burner. Explain the meaning of the following words as used in question (30) above.

i.) Burn..
....(2mks)

ii.) CD writer or burner...
....(2mks)

31) CD ROM means Compact Disc read only memory. This means that your CD ROM drive can only read the data stored on a CD. What will you use to store your own data onto a CD?.....................(1mk)

32) There are two types of CDs – Recordable and Rewritable. Explain

i.) Recordable CD...
....(2mks)

ii.) Rewritable CD...

....(2mks)

33) Write in full DVD..(1mk)

34) On most DVDs it is written 4.7GB/120min and on CDs 700MB/80min. From this information, compare DVDs and CDs?...
....(2mks)

35) Compare DVDs and Blue Ray...
....(2mks)

36) On a recordable CD it is labeled CD-R80 and on DVD it is written DVD–R. What will you find written on a rewritable CD and DVD....
....(2mks)

37) The Snipping tool is a simple screen capture tool in Windows 7. It captures screenshots with any comments you choose to associate alongside. The screenshots in Windows XP known as screen dump is done in a different way. Describe how this is done?....................
....
....
....(4mks)

38) It is always advisable to use soft shut down to turn off your computer in order to avoid damage to the configuration files. List the steps you will follow to turn off Windows 7............................
....
....
....(4mks)

39) We have heard that a computer is a very fast and accurate machine. Every day scientists try to improve on this fastness. To be fast during work, we can also use short cut keys or command buttons after mastering the main menus. Give the windows short cut keys for the following:

i.) Copy......................Cut........................Paste................(3mks)

40) In Windows 7 the shortcut **Win** means holding the **Windows key** on your keyboard. Give the outcome for the following Windows 7 short cuts:

short cuts:

i) Win + Up Arrow...

ii) Win + M ....

iii) Alt + F4 ....(3mks)

41) Name four uses of the taskbar...
....
....
....(4mks)
42) Write down the steps you will following to Quit Windows XP.........
....
....
....(4mks)
43) What is a Window?...
....(2mks)
44) Outline the differences between Windows XP operating system and
    a Window...
....
....
....(4mks)
45) Fill in the blank spaces
    a) For resizing a window you can use the ....headed arrow
       and drag to the desired size.   (1mk)
    b) ....is basically a quick link to a program, a file
       or a folder.   (1mk)
    c) Reverting a window from its original size from its maximized size
       is known as ....a window   (1mk)
    d) The icon that helps you view all the files and folders of different
       users in a local network is known as...............................(1mk)
46) Write down the steps for creating a shortcut for a program in
    Windows operating system..
....
....(3mks)
47) ....is the working area of the computer where all
    manipulations take place.   (1mk)
48) Programs on the Windows desktop are represented by graphics
    called...(1mk)
49) The screenshot below shows Microsoft Word 2013 running in a
    Window. Label the parts 1 – 11.

FILE HOME INSERT DESIGN PAGE LAYOUT REFERENCES MAILINGS REVIEW VIEW Sign in

Times New Roman 14

B I U abc x₂ x²

Paste

AaBbC AaBbC AaBbC

¶ Normal ¶ No Spac... Heading 1

Editing

Clipboard Font Paragraph Styles

PAGE 1 OF 1 0 WORDS

82%

2:28 AM
1/4/1980

1..2..

3..4..

5..6..

7..8..

9..10......................................

11..

50) What is the function of the part labelled 7?...............................

....

....

....(4mks)

51) What is a menu?...

....(2mks)

52) Many of the components in the screenshot above are similar for Office 2007, 2010, 2013, 2014 and windows applications which makes it easy for you to manage your work. Fill in the blank spaces with the appropriate elements.

i.) ....contains the window's name, the control menu and close buttons.

ii.)........................helps you increase and decrease zoom on window.

iii.)....................is used in place of minimizing, maximizing, restoring and close buttons. Can also be used to size and move a window.

iv.)......................display graphic tool buttons that represent shortcuts to various tab commands.

v.)The ....button reduces a window to a button on the taskbar.

vi.)The ....button enlarges the window to full screen.

vii.)The ....button closes the window and if a program is running in the window, exits the program.

viii.)................is a rim around the window used to resize the window.

ix.)The................bar is a bar across the bottom of the window that describes the contents of the window.

x.)The..............bar vertical or horizontal enables you to move the internal viewing area of the window.

xi.)The.................tab shows commands for saving, opening, closing etc of files if it is clicked.

A typical tab – **File tab** is shown above with its commands being Info, New, Open etc   (11mks)

53) **Tick the Correct Answer**

a) ....provides a place to type an entry, such as filename, path, font, or measurement in dialog boxes.   ☐ Textbox
        ☐ Checkbox   ☐ Filename

b) ....presents a line-up of possible options from which you can choose in dialog boxes. ☐Checkbox ☐Textbox ☐List box

c) ....is a single line list box with a drop down arrow button to the right of it in dialog boxes.   ☐Tabs
        ☐Drop down list   ☐ Command button

d) ....present a group of related choices from which you can choose one in a dialog box. ☐Options button   ☐Command button   ☐Group button

e) ....enables you to turn an option off or on in a dialog box. ☐Turn on   ☐ Check box   ☐ Option Off

f) ....button when selected in a dialog box, carries out the command displayed on the button. ☐Command ☐Display   ☐Done

g) ....represents multiple sections of a dialog box. ☐Tabs

☐Multiple ☐ Section (7mks)

54) **Complete the table below giving the description of the editing keys for text in Microsoft Word 2013.**

Key	Description
Delete	Deletes the character to the right of the insertion point
Back space	
End	
Home	
Arrow keys	
Shift+End	
Shift+Home	
Shift+Arrow key	
Ctrl+C	Copy selected text to clipboard
Ctrl+X	
Ctrl+V	

55) When you install windows based software, the installation program creates a folder for the programs to reside in on your hard disc drive. "Microsoft Office" for example, is automatically placed in a folder called.............................This is done to keep the software separate from other programs you have installed on your computer. When you create a document, spreadsheet, database, or any other file, you determine where it will reside on your.....................when you save it. If you have office 2013 installed on your PC it creates a default folder called................... When you save a document in Windows XP using one of the Microsoft Office products such as Microsoft Word or Microsoft Excel, those documents will be saved in.............................folder unless you...the program otherwise. (5mks)

56) The Window below is My Computer Window. The hard drive is partitioned into **Cornelius(C:) and Cornelius (D:)**

i) Describe how you can check the capacity of the partition Cornelius(C:)...
....
....
....(4mks)

ii) Draw the same My Computer Window with the hard disc partitioned into four (4) partitions when an additional DVD drive and a flask disk are attached...
....
....
....
....
....
....

57) Give drive letters that will always remain fixed no matter the number of drives added to your computer.

i.) Letter...Drive................................

ii.) Letter...Drive................................

iii.) Letter...Drive................................

58) A better way managing your files in Windows is by using Windows Explorer instead of My Computer Window because Windows Explorer shows your drives on the left pane and folders and files

on the right unlike the My Computer Window which shows all the drives, folders and files in the same window.

a) List the steps that you can use to start Windows Explorer...............

....

....

....

....(4mks)

b) Describe how you can create a folder using Windows Explorer.........

....

....

....(4mks)

59) Windows XP allows you to use up to 255 characters, including spaces, for your file and folder names. List all the characters that are forbidden to be used as folder or file names

i.) .... vi.) ....

ii.) .... vii.) ....

iii.) .... viii.) ....

iv.) .... ix.) ....

v.).................................... x.) ....(8mks)

60) Why are the characters above forbidden to be used in folder or file names?...

....(1mk)

Laboratory Session

Practicals: Task 1

61) Create three (3) folders using Windows Explorer on your Flask disk namely (i) Computer Science (ii) English Language (iii) Private

a)   Open Microsoft Office 2014 and type the document provided below. Use font type **Times New Roman,** font size **14pts,** line spacing **1.5,** Alignment **Justified,** heading **all caps,** font size **16pts** and font type **Bookman Old Style** and alignment **Centered.** Via Page Layout Tab, Page Setup, set margins: Top **2cm,** Bottom **2cm,** Left **2.5cm,** Right **2cm** and Gutter **0cm,** Gutter position **left.** Save the document with file name **Evolution of Computers** in the folder **Computer Science** on your flask disk.

History and Evolution of Computers

The term computer has evolved through history, resulting from man's attempt to create tools that would help him manipulate data effectively and efficiently. Each stage of change adds a function to the task performed by the previous development in this concept, giving a different definition to the term computer. It was necessary to calculate and analyze tasks employing the use of a machine. Many scientists have tried this. The seed of modern computer was sown 3500 years ago when a huge stone carved structure spread in circular pattern over the huge ground was used to perform astronomical calculations by considering the position of the sun rays.

This stone-carved structure is known as the Neolithic Computer and is the oldest computer till date. The Abacus is a calculating instrument used by the Chinese, Japanese and Koreans since ancient times. It was used in business as well as in scientific areas such as astronomical calculations, trigonometrical calculations etc. In 1942, the French mathematician Blaise Pascal invented a machine, which he called Numerical Wheel Calculator. Later the Numerical Wheel Calculator became popular as Pascaline. Although this was a remarkable achievement it had a few draw backs: In 1673 the German philosopher mathematician Gottfried Leibnitz built a mechanical calculating machine that multiplies, divides, adds and subtracts faster than Pascaline. Arithmetic capability is one of the prime functions performed by a computing device. The real beginning of computers as we know them today started with the efforts of English mathematics professor Charles Babbge. In 1821, Babbage invented a machine known as the **Difference Engine** to perform mathematical calculations. In 1832, he got an idea to develop another machine that could perform not only mathematical tasks but also any type of calculation. Soon, he began work on the new machine, and in 1856 he succeeded in developing it. The new machine was named the **Analytical Engine.** Due to his contribution in the field of computers, Charles Babbage is also known as father of modern computers.

Three American scientists - John von Neuman, Eckert and Mauchly - jointly developed the Electronic Numerical Integrator and Calculator (ENIAC) on February 19, 1946. They were commissioned by the US army ordinance department for military reasons during World War II. This project began in 1943. It was put to work on calculation for atomic bomb research at LOS Alamos, New Mexico Government Research Laboratory. ENIAC was less impressive because it needed a large amount of electric power to run, weighed some thirty tons, very large with each operation controlled by different programs which could not be stored internally as in modern computers and to change from one computer to another difficult.

In 1945, the Hungarian born mathematician John Von Neuman wrote a brilliant report describing several hardware concepts and that of stored programs. With the stored program concept, the instructions for the computer are coded and stored in the machine. Electrical signals or pulses that bear specific codes in the hexadecimal coded mode are subsequently interpreted as characters and symbols.

In 1947, he defined that computer as "a device that accepts input, process data, and stores information and produces output." The Electronic Discrete Variable Automatic Computer which Von helped invent was the first to use the stored program concept.

Mauchly and Eckert designed the Universal Automatic Computer being the first commercially available electronic or digital computer.

It was introduced in 1951 and the first one delivered to the US census bureau to tabulate census statistics. It was used to predict the 1952 US Presidential elections. Public awareness of computers increased when in 1952 the UNIVAC after analyzing only 5 per cent of the tallied votes, correctly predicted that Dwight D. Eisenhower would win the Presidential elections.

The first commercialized computers were purely used for research and database management purposes. However, as the transistor industry began making chips which could replace very large circuits, cheaper and less cumbersome computers began to surface.

Task 2

b.) Create again a new document in Microsoft Word 2010/2013/2014 etc. Type the text on page 30 using font type **Cambria,** font size **12pts,** line Spacing **1**, Alignment **Justified,** heading **all caps** font size **14pts** and font type **Calibri** and alignment **Centered.** Via Page Layout tab,

Page Setup, set margins: Top **1.5cm**, Bottom **1.5cm**, Left **2cm**, Right **1.5cm** and Gutter **0cm,** Gutter position **left. Save the document with file name <u>Advert</u> in the folder English <u>Language</u> on your flask disk.**

Ad: Ministry of Secondary Education (MINESEC) Commends Practical Computer Education by Coni T. Tawong to Cameroonians

The Ministry of Secondary Education has commended the use of a new book for Computer Science. The book titled: Practical Computer Education is published by **Tobby Vision Computers Ltd**. It is a book that seeks to make young Cameroonians not only have access to Information and Communication Technology but familiarize themselves with it and use it with ease. Practical Computer Education is a book that covers the syllabus prescribed by the Ministry of Secondary Education for students of lower Secondary Schools. It is not only going to be useful for these students but for any individual who wants to be educated on the use of computers.

It is clear that nowadays education without Computer Studies makes the individual remain myopic in the global world. Practical Computer Education is a book that has come to make students study within the shortest time operating systems and applications of the information and communication technology even without teachers in their homes. Teachers can also find this book very useful as a tool to help their students since it is a self directive book.

You can get the book in the following addresses: **Bamenda:** – Presbookshop, Standard Bookshop, Simplicity Bookshop, Mujota Bookshop, Friendship Business Centre situate at Commercial Avenue, Excellence bookshop Nkwen. **Douala:** – Presbookshops situate at Deido and New Road Bonaberi. **Kumbo:** – Presbookshop and Diplomatic bookshop situate at Squares. **Yaoundé:** – Presbookshops situate at Melen and Carrefour EMIA – Holy Infant bookshop situate at Melen. **Buea:** – Presbookshop situate Opposite Prison. **Kumba:** – Presbookshops situate at Foncha Avenue and at Fiango. **Limbe:** – Presbookshop situate at down beach **Tiko:** – Presbookshop situate before roundabout. **Wum:** – Presbookshop situate near Garanti Park. **Mamfe:** – Pressbookshop situate at Commercial Street

DISTRIBUTION

– Presbookshops' headquarter limbe

– Tobby Vision Computers Ltd

TEL.: +237 675 425 551

The book has also been selected by CreateSpace, an Amazon Company and printing has commenced to make the book available to millions of customers on Amazon.com, Amazon.co.uk, Amazon.de, Amazon.fr, Amazon.it, and Amazon.es. The book **Practical Computer Education Volume II** is also selected by thousands of major bookstores and online retailers.

Amazon's Print Company **CreateSpace** expanded channel selected the book's volume II last July 2015 and is printing paperback copies to make it available to libraries and academic institutions worldwide. This expanded channel will also make available **Practical Computer Education Volume II by Coni T. Tawong** to public libraries, elementary and secondary school libraries, and libraries at academic institutions worldwide.

CreateSpace Publisher Direct which will continue doing printing of millions of paperback copies of **Practical Computer Education Volume II** already has contracted to make it available to certified resellers such as Independent bookstores and booksellers worldwide. The **CreateSpace Direct Program** will allow eligible resellers to buy **Practical Computer Education Volume II** at wholesale prices directly from **CreateSpace** – the Amazon Print Company.

Tobby Vision Computers is taking their Computer Studies and creativity to the next level. Author and Lead Computer Studies Teacher and his team of seven are into the **School Enterprise Challenge**, and students are learning what it means to run a business while in school. Shop **Practical Computer Education Volume I and II online on Author's Amazon Page** http://www.amazon.com/Coni-T.-Tawong/e/B013YWC4OO

Practical Computer Education Volume II is a global Information and Communication Technology book for educational institutions, with the goal of making students comply with 21st century education globally, socially and responsibly in a safe and healthy environment. It was published in July 2015 by the **Cameroonian based Publisher, Tobby Vision Computers.** This book is a fantastic opportunity for students and schools to study ICTs which not only make them comply with present day education, but also inspire and develop year on year their careers.

Tobby Vision Computers is an international publisher having an ICT vocational centre working to improve the relevancy, quality, and availability of educational material resources globally. Their pioneering approach uses profit–making school–run business to teach Computer soft and hardware and ICT educational skills. This model allows its students in a community hosting The University of Bamenda and higher institutions of learning to be fully employed and hence alleviate poverty, improve the sustainability of these employers while at the same time enabling these students offer a more relevant and higher quality services.

For media enquiries and more information contact:

[Cornelius Tfurndabi Tawong, corneliustawong@gmail.com, (+237)675425551]

http://www.amazon.com/Coni-T.-Tawong/e/B013YWC4OO

Task 3

c.) Lastly, create a new document in Microsoft Word 2010/2013/2014 etc. Type an invitation letter of not more than 50 words to your friend inviting him for your birthday party using font type **Time New Roman,** font size **12pts,** line Spacing **1.5**, Alignment **Justified,** your address **Boldface and right aligned,** heading **all caps** font size **14pts** and font type **Harrington** and alignment **Centered.** Via Page Layout tab, Page Setup, set margins: Top **2cm**, Bottom **2cm**, Left **2cm**, Right **2cm** and Gutter **0cm,** Gutter position **left.** Set paper size to A4 and paper orientation to portrait. Save the document with file name **Invitation** in the folder **Private** on your flask disk.

Safely closed your flask disk, remove it and hand to your teacher for inspection, evaluation and printing.

The Screenshot below shows Windows XP Windows Explorer. Answer the questions that follow.

a) Give the name and functions of the parts labelled A–G

A..

B..

C..

D..

E..

F..

G..

62) One way to store your files or take along with you is to copy them onto flask disks, external hard discs or save on Google drive. However, when your flask disks or external hard disc is full or infected with a virus, you may want to erase it and start afresh.

a) State the procedure you would use to format a flask disk or external hard disc...
....
....

....

....

....

....(5mks)

b) Describe in your own words the procedure you would use to import pictures and videos from your digital camera to your computer.......

....

....

....(3mks)

c) What is Microsoft Paint? ....

....(1mk)

d) List the steps used to Start Microsoft Paint in Windows 7

....

....

....(3mks)

63) Most students do their drawings using the mouse in Microsoft Paint. Though it can be difficult, but practice always makes it easy. Below is a diagram showing the tools you will use most often to draw in Microsoft Paint. Name and give a function each of the parts labeled A–P.

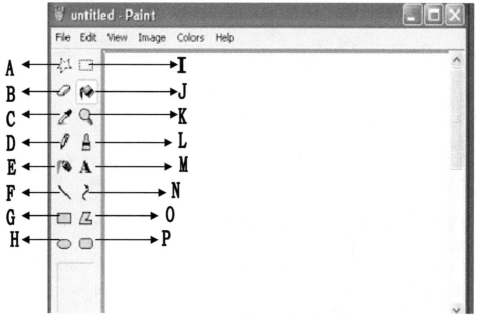

A. Name:..................................Function....................................

....

B. Name:...............................Function..................................
....
C. Name:...............................Function..................................
....
D. Name:...............................Function..................................
....
E. Name:...............................Function..................................
....
F. Name:...............................Function..................................
....
G. Name:...............................Function..................................
....
H. Name:...............................Function..................................
....
I. Name:...............................Function..................................
....
J. Name:...............................Function..................................
....
K. Name:...............................Function..................................
....
L. Name:...............................Function..................................
....
M. Name:...............................Function..................................
....
N. Name:...............................Function..................................
....
O. Name:...............................Function..................................
....
P. Name:...............................Function..................................
....

(32mks)

64) Computer users scan, copy, then edit and format their documents in Microsoft Paint? (i) According to you, what are the disadvantages with scanning..
....
....

....

....

....

....

....

....(20mks)

65) Name four other document scan–editing programs you know........

....

....

....

....(4mks)

66) Suggest what can be done by programmers of document scan–
editing programs to reduce fake documents syndrome commonly
known as 'doki' in Cameroon..

....

....

....

....

....

....

....(8mks)

Laboratory Session

Practice and Record the Procedure: Review Questions

1. How would you use the My Music Folder?......................................

....

....

....

....(5mks)

2. How would you open Windows Media Player?.................................

....

....

....

....(5mks)

3. How would you play CDs and DVDS on your PC?............................

....
....
....
....
....(5mks)

4. How would you use the Media Guide?..
....
....
....
....
....(5mks)

5. How would you copy Music from a CD, DVD or Blue Ray?.............
....
....
....
....
....(5mks)

6. How would you use the media Library?...
....
....
....
....(5mks)

7. How would you create Playlists?...
....
....
....
....
....(5mks)

8. How would you check for Player Updates?..
....
....
....
....
....(5mks)

9. How would you use the Camera Wizard..
....

....
....
....
....(5mks)

10. How would you use the My Pictures Folder..................................
....
....
....
....
....(5mks)

11. How would you view pictures with Windows Picture and Fax
    Viewer?..
....
....
....
....(5mks)

12. How would you edit a digital photo?......................................
....
....
....
....(5mks)

13. How would you rename a digital photo?....................................
....
....
....
....(5mks)

14. How would you copy a digital photo?......................................
....
....
....
....(5mks)

15. How would you move a digital photo?......................................
....
....
....
....(5mks)

16. How would you delete a digital photo?...................................

....

....

....

....(5mks)

17. How would you view photos as a slide show?.........................

....

....

....

....(5mks)

18. How would you set a slide show as your screen saver?.................

....

....

....

....(5mks)

19. How would you Email digital photos?......................................

....

....

....

....(5mks)

20. How would you use the Photo Printing Wizard?.........................

....

....

....

....(5mks)

21. How would you Order Prints online?.......................................

....

....

....

....(5mks)

22. How would you open Windows Media Player?............................

....

....

....

....(5mks)

23. How would you use My Video Folder?...
....
....
....
....(5mks)

24. How would you Open Windows Movie Maker?...........................
....
....
....
....(5mks)

25. How would you get to know the Windows Movie Maker Environment?...
....
....
....
....(5mks)

26. How would you record Audios and Videos?...............................
....
....
....
....(5mks)

27. How would you listen to Internet Radio Stations? ....
....
....
....
....(5mks)

28. How would you copy music to a CD, DVD or other device?............
....
....
....
....(5mks)

29. How would you switch between Player Modes in Windows Media Player?...

....
....
....
....(5mks)

30. How would you select different Skins in Windows Media Player?...

....
....
....
....
....(5mks)

31. How would you view visualizations in Windows Media Player?........

....
....
....
....(5mks)

32. How would you change visualizations in Windows Media Player?...

....
....
....
....(5mks)

33. How would you modify Audio, Video and Graphic Equalizer Effects?..

....
....
....
....(5mks)

34. How would you import audios and videos?...................................

....
....
....
....(5mks)

35. How would you create a new collection of your favourite songs?.....

....
....
....
....(5mks)

36. How would you play Spider Solitaire?...
....
....
....
....(5mks)

37. How would you play Internet Backgammon?...
....
....
....
....(5mks)

38. How would you play Internet Checkers?...
....
....
....
....(5mks)

39. How would you play Internet Hearts?..
....
....
....
....(5mks)

40. How would you play Internet Reversi?...
....
....
....
....(5mks)

41. How would you play Internet Spades?..
....
....
....
....(5mks)

42. How would you play Pinball?..
....
....
....
....(5mks)

Laboratory Session
Practicals: Task 4
Questions Microsoft Windows

Objective: Answer the following questions on your PC within Microsoft Windows XP/7/8 or 10. For each question write a brief description explaining how you answered the question in the spaces provided after the questions in The Students Practice Workbook. Depending on the Windows installed on your PC your procedure may vary or remain the same with the one given below.

Answer Questions 1-8 pertaining to task 4

1. On the desktop, select the **Start Menu.**

2. In the **Start Menu** select **Accessories.**

3. Open **Notepad.**

4. **Minimize** the Notepad window.

5. Bring the Notepad window back up so that it is visible.

6. **Maximize** the Notepad window.

7. **Restore** the Notepad window.

8. **Close** the Notepad window.

....
....
....
....
....
....
....

Answer Questions 9-18 pertaining to task 4

9. On the desktop, open the **Recycle Bin** icon.

10. **Arrange Icons** by **Name.**

11. **Arrange Icons** by **Origin.**

12. **Arrange Icons** by **Delete date.**

13. **Arrange Icons** by **Type**.

14. **Arrange Icons** by **Size**.

15. **Select All** Files in the folder.

16. Invert this selection.

17. **Empty** the Recycle Bin.

18. **Close** the Recycle Bin window.

....

....

....

....

....

....

....

....

Answer Questions 19-23 pertaining to task 4

19. On the **Desktop** open **My Computer; Recycle Bin,** and **My Documents**

20. Use the **Mouse** to choose **Recycle Bin** on the **Taskbar**

21. Use the **Keyboard** to choose **My computer** on the **Taskbar**

22. **Resize** the **My Computer** window

23. **Close** all three windows

....

....

....

....

....

....

....

....

Answer Questions 24-38 pertaining to task 4

24. On the desktop, use the **Start Menu** to **Explore**

25. Highlight the **Desktop**.

26. In the left pane, open **My Computer**, then open **(C:).**

27. In the right pane, open the **Program Files** folder.

28. Click the **Up One Level button**.

29. In the left pane, hide all subfolders.

30. In the left pane, show all subfolders.

31. Select **Search.**
32. **Look In** "(C:)."
33. In the "Named" box, enter "Windows."
34. Perform the **search.**
35. Scroll down the list of results.
36. Close the Windows Explorer window.
37. **Shut Down** the computer.
38. Manually turn off the **Monitor.**

....

....

....

....

....

....

....

....

Answer Questions 39-57 pertaining to task 4

39. **Create** a new folder on the desktop and call it "Ngwang's Folder."
40. Rename the folder "Agbor's Folder."
41. **Open** Agbor's Folder.
42. Inside Agbor's Folder, **Create** a folder called "Lab Results."
43. Inside Agbor's Folder, **Create** another folder called "Test Results."
44. **Copy** the test Results folder.
45. **Paste** the copy of the Test Results folder inside Agbor's Folder.
46. **Delete** the copy of the Test Results folder.
47. Move the Lab Results folder inside the Test Results folder.
48. **Cut** the Lab Results Folder.
49. **Paste** the Lab Results folder back inside Agbor's Folder.
50. Insert a flask disk to your computer's USB port
51. **Label** the flask disk Coni
52. **Format** the disk labelled Coni
53. Send Agbor's Folder to the flask disk.
54. **Delete** Agbor's Folder from the **flask disk**.
55. **Delete** Agbor's Folder from the **desktop**.

....

....

....

....

....

....

....

....

Answer Questions 56-65 pertaining to task 4

56. In the **Start Menu**, click on **Help**.

57. Select the **Index Tab**.

58. Perform a **Search** for "printers".

59. Select "troubleshooter."

60. Scroll through the Windows Troubleshooter

61. Use the **Search** to find information on printing

62. Bookmark this topic as a **Favourite**

63. Return to the **Contents** Section of **Help**

64. Locate printing quickly through **Favourites**

65. **Close** the Help window.

....

....

....

....

....

....

....

....

Answer Questions 66-82 pertaining to task 4

66. On the desktop, open the **My Computer** icon.

67. Open the **Control Panel** icon.

68. Open the **Day/Time** icon.

69. Change the month to "December."

70. Change the year to "2015."

71. Change the time to "12:38PM."
72. Change the time zone to "Mexico City."
73. Cancel these changes.
74. Open the **Fonts** icon.
75. Insert the **Toolbar**
76. Hide the **Toolbar**.
77. View the files as **Large Icons**.
78. View the files as a **List**.
79. **List Fonts by Similarity**.
80. **Select All** the fonts.
81. **Invert** your selection.
82. **Close** the Fonts window.

....
....
....
....
....
....
....

Answer Questions 83-89 pertaining to task 4

83. Open the **Multimedia** icon
84. In the **Audio Tab**, move all Playback Volumes to their highest setting
85. Move each Recording Volume to its lowest setting
86. Change the Recording Quality to **Telephone Quality**
87. In the **Video Tab**, show video in **Full Screen**
88. In the **MIDI Tab**, change the MIDI Output to **Custom Configuration**
89. Cancel these changes

....
....
....
....

....

....

Answer Questions 90-98 pertaining to the same task

90. Open the **Display** menu
91. Change the **Wallpaper** on the desktop to clouds
92. Display the **wallpaper** in **tile** format
93. **Apply** this to the desktop
94. Open the **Internet Options**
95. Change the **Homepage** to www.minesec.gov.cm
96. Set the **History** folder to 20 days
97. Change the amount of **Disk space** to use to 60 MB
98. **Cancel** these selections

....

....

....

....

....

Fill in the Blank Spaces

1. When you save your file for the first time, you will see the .... box.
2. ....option is used for printing the pages.
3. The Copy command is found on the .... of Microsoft Word 2007/2010/2013/2014.
4. ....command creates a new file.
5. To type a capital letter, press...key once to turn it on.

The Students Practice Work Book Multiple Choice Questions (MCQs)

Tick (√) the correct answer

1. A Windows7 colour scheme that changes the way Windows itself looks and behaves on your screen is called?................................
   ☐Scheme ☐Aero ☐Screen

2. The primary printer that Windows uses automatically is called?
   ☐Inkjet Printer   ☐Primary Printer   ☐Default printer

3. Windows 7's main screen that shows your program icons, the Start button, and the taskbar is called?   ☐Desktop ☐Taskbar
   ☐Default Screen

4. A file that is attached onto an e-mail message is called..................
   ☐Attachment   ☐ Message   ☐ Image

5. ....appears when you plug a memory card into your PC.
   ☐Plug box   ☐Memory box   ☐AutoPlay dialog box

6. ....is a wireless technology for adding devices to your computer.
   ☐USB   ☐Wireless tooth   ☐ Bluetooth

7. Recording content to a CD or DVD is known as.......................
   ☐Typing   ☐Burning   ☐Registering

8. ....is a folder containing multiple files that have been packed in such a way that all excess space is eliminated.
   ☐Compressed file   ☐Folder   ☐Zip drive

9. .... are tiny files that are used by Web sites to track your online activity and recognize you whenever you access the site.
   ☐Cookies   ☐Viruses   ☐themes

10. .... is a Windows tool that shows you the status of all the hardware elements on your PC.   ☐Driver Signing
    ☐Windows Update   ☐ Device Manager

11. To copy data from a main source to a peripheral device is known as..........☐Copy   ☐ Cut   ☐Download

12. To click and hold a mouse button while moving the mouse is known as..........☐Moving   ☐Dragging   ☐Clicking

13. ....is a small icon next to a URL address in an Internet browser's address bar. ☐Favicon   ☐URL   ☐Icon

14. A software or hardware device designed to block unauthorized intruders from gaining entry to an individual computer or network is called.................☐Firewall   ☐Dragging   ☐Clicking

15. A keychain–size storage unit that saves files on memory cards; you can plug it into your computer and access it like any other external hard drive is called...

☐Flask drive   ☐Memory card   ☐Card Reader

16. The combination of typeface and other qualities, such as size, pitch, and spacing, that can be applied to characters in a document is called................... ☐Line spacing   ☐Bold face ☐Font

17. A little always on Windows 7 desktop program, such as the Slide Show, Clock, Pictures, Phases of the moon are called?................... ☐Moon   ☐Gadgets   ☐Clock

18. ....refers to menu options that are currently unavailable ☐Unavailable   ☐Menu unavailable   ☐Grayed out

19. What is the technical term used when two or more pieces of electronic equipment, such as a cell phone and a Bluetooth adapter, first recognize each other? ☐Bluetooth connect ☐Handshake   ☐ Phone recognized

20. ....is a computer function by which it saves all the computer's memory then turns the computer off   ☐Hibernate ☐Shutdown   ☐ Restart

21. Is a small picture that represents an object or program................ ☐ Button   ☐Icon   ☐ Favicon

22. The blinking icon that appears on your computer screen at the location where characters you type appear called a cursor is also known as.....☐Two headed arrow ☐I beam ☐Insertion point

23. ....enable you to group related folders and files together. Windows 7 has four default libraries: Documents, Music, Pictures, and Videos.   ☐Libraries ☐Documents ☐Music

24. A computer network that spans a relatively small area or to group of buildings is called...........☐LAN   ☐TCP☐CAMTEL network

25. To identify yourself on a computer by entering a username and password is called............ ☐Log in   ☐Log name ☐User name

26. To tell Windows that you are done using the computer without actually turning off the computer is called....................... ☐Log off ☐Log out   ☐Turn off

27. To.................is to identify you on a computer by entering a user name and password. ☐Log out ☐Log on   ☐Sign in

28. A Windows 7 tool that allows you to quickly view all open windows and programs in either thumbnail or full screen mode is called................. ☐Handshake ☐Aero Peek ☐Aero tool

29. A Windows 7 feature that minimizes all windows except the one. Click on the title bar of the window you want to keep open and then drag it back and forth quickly. ☐Windows 7 Shake ☐Aero Shake ☐Minimize Shake

30. A Windows 7 feature that lets you resize a window to half its size just by dragging it to a side of the screen. ☐Aero Screen ☐Aero Snap ☐Aero drag

31. ....is a type of application that is designed to cause problems to computer systems. ☐Problem ware ☐Malware ☐Virus Ware

32. ....is the portion of the hard drive that contains the operating system which helps to start up the computer. ☐D: drive partition ☐Track O ☐Master boot record partition

33. A device that converts digital data from a computer into analog data for transmission over telephone lines by modulating it into waves is called..........................☐Modem ☐Modulator ☐Analog

34. ....is an ultra light laptop built for on-the-road Internet access and word ☐Laptop ☐Notebook ☐Palm top

35. .... is a way that Windows virtually separates parts of a drive. ☐Partition ☐Separation ☐Drive D:

36. The act of sending an e-mail to a user falsely claiming to be an established legitimate enterprise in an attempt to scam the user into surrendering private information is called............ ☐Phishing ☐Scaming ☐Spaming

37. ....is technology that Windows uses to automate hardware installation. ☐Plug and Play ☐Unplug and Play ☐Automate and Play

38. The lineup of documents waiting to be printed by your printer is called.............☐ Print queue ☐Prints waiting ☐Ready to Print

39. ....is a tool that enables you to record exactly what your computer is doing so that you can show whoever you've asked for

technical help. ☐Snipping tool ☐Problem Steps Recorder ☐Sound Recorder

40. To copy music from a CD to your PC using Windows Media Player is known as........... ☐Transfer ☐Ripping ☐Copying

41. A storage technology that tends to run faster and cooler with simpler connections. ☐External hard disc ☐Hard disc drive ☐SATA hard drive

42. ....is a tab-based interface for Microsoft-based applications, such as Microsoft Office 2014, that contains all the primary commands. ☐Scenic Ribbon ☐Quick Access Ribbon ☐Interface Ribbon

43. A program that searches the Internet for specified keywords and returns a list of the Web pages where the keywords were found is called........................... ☐Search engine ☐Internet search ☐Web search

44. ....is a Windows 7 built-in tool for creating screen shots. ☐Print Screen ☐Shots tool ☐Snipping tool

45. Any unsolicited e-mail is called...................................
☐Scam ☐Spam ☐Bulk mail

46. Any software that covertly gathers user information through the user's Internet connection without his or her knowledge, usually for advertising purposes is called.........
☐Scamming ☐Spamming ☐Spyware

47. The command which uses restore points to return your PC to a point where it worked properly is called....................... ☐System Reg ☐System Restore ☐Restore Point

48. SATA hard drive is a new technology. Give the full meaning of SATA... ☐Secure and technical Arrangement ☐Safe and Accurate Arrangement ☐Serial Advanced Technology Attachment

49. The thick blue bar that runs across the top of a window is called................☐title bar ☐menu bar ☐standard bar

50. A power strip combined with a battery to keep your computer running when the power goes out is called.....................
☐Battery ☐UPS ☐System Battery

51. A computer connection that you can use to attach many different kinds of devices and peripherals to a computer is called........................□PS2 □USB □COM ports

52. A Windows tool that automates common processes, such as adding software or setting up a network is called a ....
□Wizard □Witch □Computer witch

53. Wifi stands for wireless fidelity, a broad ban connection used to log onto the Internet. If present, provides a _____ in bookstores, computer stores, coffee stores □hotspot □bluetooth □blue ray

Chapter Three
Word Processing

1. What is Microsoft Office?...
....
....
....(2mks)

2. When you purchase Microsoft Office 2013 or its license you basically purchase the right to install and use the...............programs?
....
....
....
....
....
....
....
....(3mks)

3. When you purchase Microsoft Office 2014 or its license you basically purchase the right to install and use.....................programs?
....
....
....
....
....
....
....
....(3mks)

3b. Name four other versions of Microsoft Office.................................

....
....
....
....(2mks)

4. State the steps you will use to start Microsoft Word 2014 in Windows 7..
....
....
....
....
....
....
....(3mks)

5. When typing in Microsoft Word, the flashing line on your Window is called..It indicates where the text you type will... As you are typing, Microsoft Word automatically ....text to the next line.   (3mks)

6. Name four tabs in Microsoft Word 2013..
....
....
....(4mks)

7. Describe how you can create a new tab named **Chantal** in Microsoft Word 2013
....
....
....
....
....(8mks)

8. Most of those who begin by using shortcuts get blocked-up because if the tab is not available they will not know what to do. What is your advice to computer beginners?...
....
....
....
....
....(4mks)

9. Describe how you can get to all the commands found in Microsoft Word 2013...
....
....
....(4mks)

10. How do you get to all commands in Microsoft Word 2007/2010/2013/2014 etc?
....
....
....
....
....(4mks)

11. The secret concerning location of commands in all versions of Microsoft Word is to check for the Customize command.
a.) State how you would access the customize command in Microsoft Word 2014...
....
....(2mks)
b.) State the steps you would use to access the customize command in Microsoft Word 2013...
....
....
....(2mks)

12.When entering text in Microsoft Word Window, Microsoft Word underlines wrong grammar with.................................and wrong spellings with ....(2mks)

13. Why are local names which are correctly spelled underlined with wavy red lines?..(1mk)

14. How can you stop correctly spelled local names from being underlined with wavy redlines in Microsoft Word?..............................
....
....(2mks)

15. Give the meaning of the following found on the Microsoft Word 2003 Status bar which is located at the bottom of the document window.

(i)Page 1 ....

(ii) Sec 1 ....

(iii) 1/20 ....

(iv) At 2cm...

(v) Ln..

(vi) Col...

.... (6mks)

16. List down steps to preview a document in any version of Microsoft Word before printing..

....

....

....

....(2mks)

17. List down various ways of printing a document in any version of Microsoft Word...

....

....

....

....

....

....

....

....

....

....

....

....(8mks)

18. What do you understand by the term formatting text?...................

....

....

....(2mks

19. What will you do to display page numbering at the bottom of the page?...

....

....(2mks)

20. Write down the three basic steps required to create a Mail Merge Project in Microsoft Word 2014...
....
....
....
....
....
....
....(6mks)
21. Define Data Source in Mail Merge..(1mk)
22. Write the steps for creating a new address list for mail merge in Word 2014...
....
....
....
....
....(3mks)
23. Explain the various options for selecting the starting document for mail merge...
....
....
....
....(2mks)
24. What is a main document? ....

....
....(1mk)
25. What is the Thesaurus?...
....(1mk)

Multiple Choice Questions (MCQs)
Microsoft Word 2007/2010/2013/2014
Tick (√) the right answer
26. The only way to change print margins for a document is to enter the margins in the Page Set Up dialog box
　　　☐True　　　　　☐False

27. What button is this picture showing? A ⌄
- ☐Font colour ☐Fong Size ☐Change case

28. What button is this? AB^1
- ☐Footnotes and Endnotes ☐Headers and Footers
- ☐Index and Tables

29. Under what Tab is the button located
- ☐Home tab References☐ tab ☐View tab

30. What button is this?
- ☐Format Painter ☐Brush ☐Paste

31. Under which tab is this button found?
- ☐Home tab ☐References tab ☐View tab

32. To open an existing document, access the open command by clicking the....................which displays the................................
- ☐Office button; File Menu
- ☐Quick Access Toolbar; Open button
- ☐Insert Tab; Open Group

33. The first time you save a document you must name the file.
- ☐False ☐True

34. When you type new text in Microsoft Word ....mode replaces existing text.
- ☐Insert ☐AutoType ☐Replacement

35. Which button is used to save our documents?
- ☐Home button ☐Save Button ☐Insert button

36. Which tab on the Ribbon is found the Find command used to locate a word or phrase in the document?
- ☐Home tab ☐Insert tab ☐Review tab

37. Which tab on the Ribbon do we use to change our font size?
- ☐Home tab ☐Mailings tab ☐Font tab

38. What is Microsoft Word?
- ☐It is a typing tool
- ☐It is a calculating tool
- ☐It is a computerized tool

39. Which tab on the Ribbon do we used to cut and paste?
- ☐Home tab ☐Paste tab ☐Edit tab

40. Choose the best definition of a Mail Merge

☐Combining your school's mailroom with email technology

☐ The process of merging two documents into new documents

☐A process of bulk printing addressed envelopes

41. You can use Microsoft Word to create

☐Brochures ☐Software ☐Programs

42. In a Mail Merge operation, which of the following might represent the main document? ☐Sales brochures ☐A Form Letter ☐A Database of Names and Addresses

43. The ....indents only the first line in a paragraph

☐First Line Indent ☐Hanging Indent ☐Left Indent

44. A.............................is a popular design element used to begin in a newsletter, magazine or other publication.

☐Drop Cap ☐Alignment ☐First Line Indent

45. The simplest way to rearrange text in your document is to.....................

☐Cutting, copying and pasting.

☐Drag and drop.

☐Type and Replace

46. Keyboard shortcut for CUT command is...................................

☐Ctrl + Z ☐Ctrl + Y ☐Ctrl + X

47. Keyboard shortcut for COPY command is.....................................

☐Ctrl + Y ☐Ctrl + B ☐Ctrl + C

48. Keyboard shortcut for PASTE command is..................................

☐Ctrl + V ☐Ctrl + Y ☐Ctrl + X

49. To select a word double click...

☐anywhere over the word

☐on the left margin

☐on the right margin

50. To select a line, position the mouse pointer on the left margin near the line and ☐Click ☐Right click ☐Double click

51. Keyboard shortcut for Select All is..

☐Ctrl + A ☐Ctrl + All ☐Ctrl + Z

52. To select a sentence press hold ....while clicking anywhere over the sentence then release...

☐Ctrl ☐Alt ☐Shift

53. To select a paragraph - position the mouse pointer anywhere over the paragraph and then quickly...

☐treble click ☐double click ☐click two times

54. Your father misplaced his reading glasses and he needs to update a Word Document. What will he do?

☐Ask someone else to update the spreadsheet

☐Increase the resolution so all the screen elements are larger

☐Increase the magnification by selecting an appropriate value from the Zoom box

55. Which tab on the Ribbon above is used to layout the page of in a document?

☐Home tab ☐Page Layout tab ☐Review tab

56. Which tab is the Microsoft Word screenshot below showing?

☐Home tab ☐References tab ☐ View tab

57. Which tab is the Microsoft Word screenshot below showing?

☐View tab ☐Page Layout tab ☐Review tab

58. Which tab is the Microsoft Word screenshot below showing?

☐Mailings tab   ☐Insert tab   ☐Developer tab

59. You use Insert tab to put Header and Footer in a document.

    ☐True   ☐False

60. You cannot save your document either in a pen drive or in a diskette   ☐True   ☐False

61. To insert Pictures, you need to go to Insert tab then click Pictures

    ☐True   ☐False

62. Be careful when you delete text from a document, because after you deleted or choose Cut, the data is gone and you cannot get it back

    ☐True   ☐False

63. To create a new document in Microsoft Word 2013 you ....

☐Click on Home tab, select New

☐Click on File tab, select New

☐Click on New tab, select New

54. State the keyboard shortcut use to save a document

    ☐Ctrl + S   ☐Ctrl + Shift + S   ☐Ctrl + Alt + S

The Students Practice Work Book: More Questions

1. State the steps you will use to setup your page before you begin typing in either of the following:

a.) Microsoft Word 2007/2010/2013/2014..

....

....

....

....

....

....

....(6mks)

b.) List the steps you will use to apply bullets, numbering, and borders to selected text..

....

....

....

....

....

....(6mks)

2.) State the steps you will use to save an unnamed document in a named version of Microsoft Word.

....

....

....

....

....

....

....

....

....(8mks)

3.) With the version chosen in (2) above, say how you can check spellings and errors in grammar in a document?

....

....

....

....

....

....

....

....

....(8mks

4. Thesaurus is used to check for synonyms and antonyms. Give 8 other synonyms of the word **Nice**

(i)...(ii)..

(iii)..(iv)..

(v)...(vi)..

(vii)..(viii)...............................(8mks)

5.) State the functions of Find and Replace Command...................

....

....

....

....

....

....

....(6mks)

a.) In which tab can Find and Replace be accessed in Microsoft Word 2013?... (1mk)

b.) In which Menu can it be accessed in Microsoft Word 2003 ....(1mk)

6.) Autocorrect corrects every wrong word as you type in Microsoft Word and replaces it with the right one. How can you add local names to autocorrect...

....

....

....

....

....

....(6mks)

7.) Give three facilities of autocorrect?.......................................

....

....

....

....(3mks)

8. What is meant by Line Spacing?...
....(1mk)

9. The table below shows the description for different types of Line Spacing. Fill the appropriate Line Spacing in the table below to the corresponding description.

LINE SPACING	DESCRIPTION
e.g. At Least	Minimum line spacing that Microsoft Word can adjust to accommodate larger font sizes or graphics that would not otherwise fit within the specified spacing.
	Line spacing that is increased or decreased by a percentage that you specify.
	Line spacing for each line that accommodates the largest font in that line plus a small amount of extra space. The amount of extra space varies depending on the font used.

	Fixed line spacing that Microsoft Word does not adjust. This option makes all lines evenly spaced.
	Line spacing for each line that is one-and-one-half times that of a single line spacing.
	Line spacing for each line is twice that of single line spacing.

(6mks)

10. List the steps to insert columns in a document in Microsoft Word

....

....

....

....

....(5mks)

11. Explain the use of these commands found on the Print dialog box

All...

....

Current Page...

....

Selection...

....

Pages...

....(4mks)

12. What are headers and footers?...

....(2mks)

13. State how you would insert headers and footers into a document?..

....

....

....(2mks)

14. What are Tabs Stops?..

....

....

....(2mks)

15. What is the default Tabs Stops unit in Microsoft Word?.........(1mk)

16. How can you set Tabs Stops to 5cm?...
....(2mks)

17. What are footnotes and endnotes?...
....
....(2mks)

18. What is an index?..
....(2mks)

19. When you start adding words to the index in Microsoft Word, paragraph marks will appear. State the steps you can follow to display paragraph marks for Microsoft Word 2007/2010/ 2013?...
....
....
....
....(4mks)

20. State the steps you would use to show page boundaries in Microsoft Word 2007/2010/2013?
....
....
....
....(4mks)

a.) Name the range of other Microsoft Word options which you can customize?...
....
...:...
....
....
....
....
....
....
....
....
....
....

....

....

....(4mks)

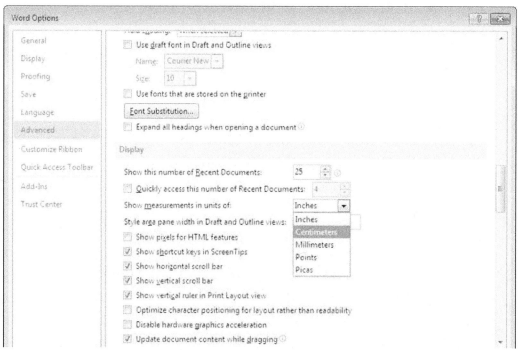

b.) You can click on File tab, Options in Microsoft Word 2007/2010/ 2013 or Tools Menu, Options in Microsoft Word 2003. In the example above I have used Microsoft Word 2013 i.e. click File tab, Selecting Options and in the Microsoft Word Options dialog box that appears I have chosen **Advanced** options and chose to show measurement in units of: **Centimeters.** With this I worked all through in Microsoft Word in measurement in units of centimeters. The **Advanced** options dialog box is shown above.

21. Identify three options each which you can also activate in Microsoft Word Options via the following:

(i) General Options...

....

....

....(3mks)

(ii) Advanced Options...

....

....

....(3mks)

(iii) Proofing Options...

....

....

....(3mks)

(iv) Language Options...

....

....

....(3mks)

22. To set automatic hyphenation, click on the ....tab, click on the hyphenation button with the ....section and ....tab and then on the automatic command.
(3mks)

23. What are normal quotes and smart quotes?...........................

....

....

....(2mks)

24. Type the text **Bravo,** put normal quotes on the word then type another text **I come from Tangmbo Division** and put smart quotes.

....

....

....(2mks)

25. What is text wrap?..

....(1mk)

26. Name five text wrap options. You can get wrap options by right clicking the object, selecting format object, then choosing Layout tab.

....

....

....

....

....(5mks)

27. What is Word Art? ....

....(1mk)

a.) The Word Art icon is found on the ....tab(1mk)

28. What are Microsoft Word Styles?...
....(1mk)

29. When you apply Microsoft Word styles to headings, sub headings and other aspects of your document, you can easily insert a table of contents, table of figures, table of authorities etc. The screenshot below shows the Home tab of Microsoft Word 2013

document with styles. Using this Home tab, describe how you will perform the following:

(i) Insert automatic Table of Contents into a document.........................
....
....
....
....
....(5mks)

(ii) Insert automatic Table of Figures into a document.........................
....
....
....
....
....(5mks)

(iii) Describe how you would Insert Table of Index into a document......
....
....

....
....
....
....
....
....
....
....
....
....
....
....
....
....
....(10mks)

31. The default template file in Microsoft Word is called?.....................
....(1mk)

32. What are templates?...
....(1mk)

33. How are columns inserted in Microsoft...
....
....
....
....
....
....
....
....(5mks)

Laboratory Session
Practicals: Task 5
1. Open a new document. Insert a header "**North West Fons Union**"

Format the header to font size 10, align it center and make it boldface with font type Bookman Old Style. At the left alignment in the header insert an auto date, and an auto time…………………………...…(10mks)

2. Create a folder called **NOWEFU**. Save the document as **"Letter head"** in the folder **NOWEFU**. ……………………………………...…(5mks)

3. Using the Mail Merging option, merge the document **"Invitation"** below to the addresses underneath, Save as **"Fundraising"** in the folder **NOWEFU**.

INVITATION

The Fons of the North West Region, Cameroon under the banner of North West Fons Union (NOWEFU) cordially invite

_____

to a Grand Fund Raising in view of the Completion of the frontage of their Secretariat in Nkwen-Bamenda scheduled for
SATURDAY, December 26th 2015
at the
Bamenda Congress Hall
The Grand Fund Raising shall begin with a Divine Service at 9:00am prompt
Signed:_____
Senator Fon Teche Njei
Fon of Ngienmuwah

Addresses
1. H. E. Peter Agbor TABI
   Assistant Secretary General
   Presidency of the Republic of Cameroon
2. H. E. Philemon YANG
   Prime Minister and Head of Government
   The Republic of Cameroon
3. Prof Peter LANGEH ABETY
   Chairman Board of Directors
   Cameroon GCE Board
4. Prof TAFAH EDOKAT Edward

Vice Chancellor, The University of Bamenda

5. Dr. Nick NGWANYAM

Chief Executive Officer, St. Louis University Institute Bamenda

6. Coni T. TAWONG

Chief Executive Officer, Tobby Vision Computers Ltd Bamenda

(30mks)

Laboratory Session

Task 6

1.) Reproduce the text **"Ad"**, **Task 2** on page 30......................(46mks)

2.) Save your work as **"Ad 2"**..(2mks)

3.) Print a copy of **"Ad 2"** ....(2mks)

Laboratory Session

Task 7

1. Type the text "**Ad**", **Task 2** on page 30 as fast as you can, using the font size 14, and 1.5 line spacing................................(15mks)

2. Set the paper size to A4 and left and right margins at 2.5cm and 2cm respectively, top and bottom margins at 2cm respectively, gutter at 0 and gutter position left then justify the text..........(6mks)

3. Save your work as **"Advert"** and print one copy...................(3mks)

4. Change the line spacing to single...(1mk)

5. Change the font type of the heading to Bookman Old Style and the font size to 24pts...(4mks)

6. The Thesaurus is found in Microsoft Word 2013 under Review/Proofing tab. Use the Thesaurus and look up the synonyms of the word **commend** as used in the "Ad" on **Task 2, page 30** and replace it with any synonym of your choice.........................(3mks)

7. Indent the first line of the first paragraph by 1.27cm.............(2mks)

8. Indent the second paragraph from the left and right by 2cm each, and change the text of the paragraph to Italics....................(6mks)

9. Select the first letter of the first paragraph and apply Drop Cap

(1mk)

10. Insert page numbers, place page numbers at bottom and center of page and make them boldface..(4mks)

11. Save your work as **"Ad 3"** in your flask disk in the folder **"practicals"**. Create this folder using the Save As dialog box...(5mks)
12. Print two copies..(1mk)

Laboratory Session
Task 7
34. Reproduce the Table on page 73 below to be exact in any version of Microsoft Word..(30mks)
a.) Describe how you merged the cells in row two....................(2mks)
b) Fill the empty with shading colour green.............................(2mks)
c.) Type the numbers 1–10 in the empty cells and center the numbers vertically and align to the right side of the cells.......................(5mks)
d.) Print one copy

....
....
....
....
....
....
....
....
....
....
....
....
....
....
....
....
....
....
....
....

REPUBLIQUE DU CAMEROUN
Paix–Travail–Patrie
Ministere des enseignements Secondaires

REPUBLIC OF CAMEROON
Peace–Work–Fatherland
Ministry of Secondary Education

INFORMATION AND COMMUNICATION TECHNOLOGIES 2
PI AND JU INTERNATIONAL ANGLO SAXON COLLEGE YAOUNDE
General Certificate of Education Mock Examination

JUNE 2015   **ORDINARY LEVEL**

Subject Title	**Information and Communication Technologies**
Paper No	**Paper 2 – Practical**
Subject Code No.	**5176**

One and a half hours

Action	Keyboard	Mouse	Right Mouse	Tab
Remove text emphasis	Select text to be changed			
	Ctrl + B (remove bold)	Click the appropriate button: B I U	Format cells	Format cells
			Select the Home tab, Font and click **Regular** in the Font dialog box	
Auto Sum	Place the insertion point where you want the sum of figures to appear and click *fx* Formula			
Restore deleted input	**Crtl + Z**	Click: the Undo button		
Rows, adding	Select the row by right clicking in the row reference box (at the side of row)			
			Insert	**Insert, Rows**
Rows, deleting	Select the row by right clicking in the row reference box (at the side of row)			
			Delete	Delete, Rows
Save	**Crtl + S**	**Click on File tab, Save**		**File tab, Save**
	If you have not already saved the file you will be prompted to specify the directory and to name the file. If you have already done this, then Microsoft Word will automatically save it.			
Save using different name or to a different folder				**File tab, Save As**
	Select the appropriate drive or folder and change the filename if relevant. Click on **File** tab, Save.			

Laboratory Session
Task 8

35. Auto shape Drawings and Pictures

A.) Here are some Autoshapes, Clip Arts and Pictures

Tobby Vision Computers Students

i.) Draw a rectangle. Set the shape fill and outline fill with green colour.

(i–a) Copy the rectangle and paste close to the first one. Set shape fill outline and outline fill with red colour. Copy again the rectangle and paste close to the second. Set shape fill and outline fill with yellow colour. Draw a star and set shape fill and outline fill with colour gold. Place the star on the red strip i.e. the second rectangle. Holding down the shift key on your keyboard, click on all three rectangles and star. Right click on the selected rectangles and star and choose group. This gives you the Cameroon flag. Note other skills discovered during the exercise on The Students Practice Workbook below. Import and work on JPEG pictures then record any skills discovered...........................

....

....

....

....

....

....

....

....(20mks)

ii.) Why do we group autoshapes, pictures and clip arts?...................

....

....

....

....

....

....

....(4mks)

36. What is water mark?...

....(1mk)

37. Describe how you would you insert a picture water mark into the document "**Ad**", **Task 2** on page 30...

....

....

....

....(5mks)

38. Describe how you would insert a text water mark into the document "**Ad**", **Task 2** on page 30...

....

....

....

....(5mks)

39. Explain what kind of document you would insert a water mark into and how you would insert either text or picture water mark?.........

....

....

....

....

....

....

....

....

....(10mks)

40. What do you understand by Mail Merge Helper?...........................

....(1mk)

41. State the six steps used in the Mail Merge Wizard ....

....

....

....

....

....

....

....

....

....

....

....

....

....
....
....
....
....
....
....
....
....
....
....
....
....
....
....
....
....(12mks)

The Students Practice Work Book: Multiple Choice Questions

Tick (√) the Right Answer(s)

1.) Which of the following is not a valid version of Microsoft Office?

        A. ☐Office XP   B. ☐Office Vista

        C. ☐Office 2014   D. ☐None of the above

2.) You cannot close Microsoft Word by

    A. ☐clicking on Office button then Exit

    B. ☐pressing Alt + F4

    C. ☐clicking X button on the title bar

    D. ☐clicking on Office button, Choosing Close

3.) The Keyboard key F12 opens the ....

    A. ☐Save As dialog box

    B. ☐Open dialog box

    C. ☐Save dialog box

    D. ☐Close dialog box

4.) What is the keyboard shortcut key to open the Open dialog box?

    A.☐F12   B.☐ Shift F12

C. ☐ Alt + F12   D. ☐ Ctrl + F12

5.) Pressing F8 key on the keyboard three times selects
    A. ☐ a word   B. ☐ a sentence
    C. ☐ a paragraph D. ☐ the entire document

6.) To select a word
    A. ☐ press Ctrl + A   B. ☐ double-click on the word
    C. ☐ press Alt + A   D. ☐ press Shift + A

7.) What happens if you press Ctrl + Shift + F8 on your keyboard?
    A. ☐ It activates extended selection
    B. ☐ It activates the rectangular selection
    C. ☐ It selects the paragraph on which the insertion line is
    D. ☐ None of above

8.) How can you disable extended selection mode?
    A. ☐ Press F8 again to disable   B. ☐ Press Delete to disable
    C. ☐ Press ESC to disable   D. ☐ Press Enter to disable

9.) What is the maximum number of lines you can set for a Drop Cap?
    A. ☐ 3   B. ☐ 10   C. ☐ 15   D. ☐ 20

10.) What is the default number of lines to drop for Drop Cap?
    A. ☐ 3   B. ☐ 10   C. ☐ 15   D. ☐ 20

11.) What is the shortcut key you can press to create a copyright symbol?
    A. ☐ Alt+Ctrl+C   B. ☐ Alt + C   C. ☐ Ctrl + C
    D. ☐ Ctrl+Shift+C

12.) How many columns can you insert in a Word document at maximum?
    A. ☐ 35   B. ☐ 45   C. ☐ 55   D. ☐ 65

13.) What is the smallest and largest font size available in Font size tool box on the Home tab?   A. ☐ 8 and 72   B. ☐ 8 and 64
    C. ☐ 12 and 72   D. ☐ None of above

14.) What is the maximum font size you can apply for any character?
    A. ☐ 163   B. ☐ 1638   C. ☐ 16038
    D. ☐ None of above

15.) Which of the following is graphics solution for Microsoft Word?
    A. ☐ Clipart   B. ☐ WordArt
    C. ☐ Drop Cap   D. ☐ All of the above

16.) The keystroke Ctrl + I is used to ....

A. ☐Increase font size   B. ☐Inserts a line break

C. ☐Indicate the text should be bold

D. ☐Applies italic format to selected text

17.) A character that is raised and smaller above the baseline is known as:

A. ☐Outlined   B.☐ Raised

C. ☐Superscript   D.☐ Subscript

18.) What is the purpose of inserting header and footer in a document?

A. ☐To enhance the overall appearance of the document

B. ☐To mark the starting and ending of page

C. ☐To make large document more readable

D. ☐To allow page headers and footers appear on document when printed

19.) Which of the following function keys activates the spelling checker?   A. ☐F5   B.☐ F7   C.☐ F9   D.☐ Shift + F7

20.) The minimum number of rows and columns in Microsoft Word document is....... A. ☐1 and 2   B. ☐2 and 1   C. ☐2 and 2   D. ☐None of above

21.) The Thesaurus tool in Microsoft Word is used for

A. ☐Spelling suggestions   B. ☐Grammar options

C. ☐Synonyms and Antonyms of words   D. ☐All of the above

22.) Why are Drop Caps used in documents?

A. ☐To drop all the capital letters

B. ☐To automatically begin each paragraph with a capital letter

C. ☐To begin a paragraph with a large dropped initial capital letter

D. ☐None of the above

23.) A bookmark is an item or location in a document that you identify as a name for future reference. Which of the following task is accomplished by using bookmarks?

A. ☐To add anchors in web pages

B. ☐To mark the ending of a paragraph of document

C. ☐To quickly jump to specific location in document

D. ☐To add hyperlinks in webpage

24.) A Word Processor is most likely used to

A. ☐Keep an account of money spent

B. ☐Do a computer search in media center

C. ☐Maintain an inventory

D. ☐Type a manual

25.) Where can you find the horizontal split bar on Microsoft Word Window?

A. ☐On the left of horizontal scroll bar

B. ☐On the right of horizontal scroll bar

C. ☐On the top of vertical scroll bar

D. ☐On the bottom of vertical scroll bar

26.) Which of the following is not available on the Ruler of Microsoft Word Window

A. ☐Tab stop box   B. ☐Left indent

C. ☐Right indent   D. ☐Center indent

27.) What is place to the left of horizontal scroll bar in Microsoft Word?

A. ☐Tab stop buttons   B. ☐View buttons

C. ☐Split buttons   D. ☐Indicators

28.) Which file starts Microsoft Word?

A. ☐Winword.exe   B. ☐Word.exe

C. ☐MSword.exe   D. ☐Word2007.exe

29.) If you want to keep track of different editions of a document which features will you use?

A. ☐Editions   B. ☐Versions

C. ☐Track change   D. ☐All of the above

30.) How many ways can you save a document?

A.☐ 3   B.☐ 4   C.☐ 5   D.☐ 6

31.) Background colour or effects applied on a document is not visible in......................

A. ☐Web layout view   B. ☐Print layout view

C. ☐Reading view   D. ☐Print Preview

32.) What is a portion of a document in which you set certain page formatting options?

A. ☐Page   B. ☐Document   C.☐ Section   D. ☐Page Setup

33.) Borders can be applied to:

A. ☐Cells   B. ☐Document   C. ☐Text   D.☐ All of above

34.) Which of the following is not a type of page margin?

A. ☐Left   B. ☐Right   D. ☐Center   D. ☐Top

35. What is gutter margin?

A. ☐Margin that is added to the left margin when printing

B. ☐Margin that is added to the right margin when printing

C. ☐Margin that is added to the binding side of page when printing

D ☐Margin that is added to the outside of the page when printing

36.) Portrait and Landscape are...

    A. ☐Page Orientation   B. ☐Paper Size

    C. ☐Page Layout   D. ☐All of above

37.) If you need to change the typeface of a document, which tab will you choose?

    A. ☐Page Layout   B. ☐View Tab

    C. ☐Home Tab   D. ☐Mailings Tab

38.) Which of the following is not a font style?

    A. ☐Bold   B. ☐Italics   C. ☐Regular D. ☐Superscript.

39. What happens when you click Insert, and select Picture?

    A. ☐It inserts a clipart picture into a document

    B. ☐It lets you choose clipart to insert into a document

    C. ☐The Insert Picture dialog box appears

    D. ☐None of the above

40.) From which tab can you insert Header and Footer?

    A. ☐Home tab   B. ☐Insert tab

    C. ☐Mailings tab   D. ☐Reference tab

41.) When inserting page number in footer it appeared 1 but you wish to show a. How can you do that?

    A. ☐Click on Page layout tab and specify required setting

    B. ☐From Page layout tab chose Page Number and specify necessary setting

    C. ☐Click on Insert Tab, Page Number and specify required setting

    D. ☐All of the above

42.) To get the 'Symbol' dialog box, click the ....tab and choose 'Symbol'.

    A. ☐Insert tab   B. ☐Home tab

    C. ☐References tab   D. ☐Mailings tab

43.) If you want to convert a symbol or several lines of text into an Auto Correct entry, you should:

A. ☐Insert the symbol or type the text in a Word document first. Then, select the text or symbol and go to the Auto Correct dialog box - Office button, Word Options, Proofing then Auto Correct Options button.

B. ☐Click the Home tab and choose Auto Correct Options. Then, click the Insert tab and choose symbol to add the symbol or paragraph to Auto Correct.

C. ☐Auto Correct can only accommodate one line of text. It is not possible to convert a symbol or multiple lines of text into an Auto Correct entry.

D. ☐Insert the symbol or type text in a Word document first. Then, select the text or symbol and click the Insert tab followed by text box. Select Alphabetic quote and type.

44.) Auto Correct was originally designed to replace..................words as you type.

    A. ☐Short, repetitive   B. ☐Grammatically incorrect

    C. ☐Misspelled   D. ☐None of the above

45.)In Microsoft Word the mailing list is known as the ....

    A. ☐Data sheet   B. ☐Source C. ☐Data source D. ☐Sheet

46.) Which of the following is not one of the three 'Mail Merge Helper' steps?

    A. ☐Merge the two files   B.☐ Create the main document

    C. ☐Set the mailing list parameters D.☐ Create the data source

47.)Which of the following button will you add, delete, or change records in your Data Source?

    A. ☐'Data Source' button   B. ☐'Edit' button

    C. ☐'Edit Data Source' button   D. ☐'Data editing' button

48.) It is possible to ....a data source before performing a merge

    A. ☐Create   B. ☐Modify

    C. ☐Sort   D. ☐all of the above

49.) What is the default font size of a new Word document based on Normal template?

    A. ☐10pt   B. ☐12pt C. ☐14pt D.☐ None of above

50.) What is the default font used in Microsoft Word documents?

    A. ☐Times New Roman   B. ☐ Arial Black

    C. ☐Algerian   D. ☐Bookman Old Style

51.) Which tab in Font dialog box contains options to apply Font effects?

    A. ☐Font tab   B. ☐Character spacing

    C. ☐Text effects   D. ☐Home tab

52.) If you need to double underline a word, how will you do that?

A. ☐Go to Home tab and then Font option, Open Underline Style and choose Double Underline

B. ☐From Home tab choose Font option and then from Font dialog box open Underline Style and select

C. ☐Select the text the Click Home tab, Font and on Font dialog box open Underline Style and choose Double Underline.

D. ☐Click Double underline tool on the Quick Access tool bar

53.) Drop Cap means……………………………….

    A. ☐All caps   B. ☐Small Caps

    C. ☐Title case   D. ☐None of above

54.) What is the shortcut key to Font dialog box?

    A. ☐Ctrl + F   B. ☐Alt+Ctrl+F

    C. ☐Ctrl + D   D. ☐Ctrl+Shift+D

55.) How can you access the Print dialog box with keystrokes?

    A. ☐Ctrl +S   B. ☐Ctrl+Shift+ S

    C. ☐Ctrl+P   D. ☐Ctrl + Shift + P

56.) How can you make a selected letter superscripted with keystrokes?

    A. ☐Ctrl + =   B. ☐Ctrl + Shift + =

    C. ☐Alt + Ctrl + Shift + =   D. ☐None of the above

57.) What does Ctrl + = key effect to selected text?

    A. ☐Superscript   B. ☐Subscript

    C.☐ All Caps   D. ☐Shadow

58.) What happens if you mark on Hidden check box of Font dialog box after you select some text?

A. ☐The text is deleted from the document and you need to bring from Recycle bin if required again.

B. ☐The text is hidden and you need to bring it by removing the check box if needed again.

C. ☐The text is deleted and cannot be returned back

D. ☐The text is hidden and cannot be returned back.

58.) How can you increase the font size of selected text by one point every time?

    A. ☐By pressint Ctrl +]   B. ☐By pressing Ctrl + [

    C. ☐By pressing Ctrl + {   D. ☐By pressing Ctrl + }

59.) Which of the following line spacing is invalid?

    A. ☐Single   B. ☐Double   C.☐ Triple D. ☐Multiple

60.) How can you apply exactly the same formatting you did to another text?

    A. ☐Copy the text and paste in new location. Then type the new text again.

    B. ☐Copy the text and click on Paste Special command on new place

    C. ☐Select the text then click on Format Painter and select the new text.

    D. ☐All of the above.

61.) What should you do if you require pasting the same format in many places?

A.☐Click the Format Painter and go on pasting in many places holder Alt key

B.☐Double click the Format Painter then go on pasting in many places

C.☐Click the Format Painter then go on pasting to many places holding Ctrl key

D. ☐All of the above

62.) On which tab can you find the Format Painter tool button?

    A. ☐Home   B. ☐Insert

    C. ☐Mailings   D. ☐Review

63.) Which indent marker controls all the lines except first line?

    A. ☐Left indent marker   B. ☐Left indent marker

    C. ☐Hanging indent marker   D. ☐Right indent marker

64.) How can you remove Tabs Stops markers from ruler?

    A. ☐Double click the tab marker and choose Clear All

    B. ☐Drag the tab stop marker out of the ruler

    C. ☐Right click the tab stop marker and choose remove

    D. ☐All of above

65.) Which operation will you perform if you need to move a block of text?

A. ☐Copy and Paste   B. ☐Cut and Paste
C. ☐Paste and Delete   D. ☐Paste and Cut

66.) What is the extension of Word files?

A. ☐FIL   B. ☐DOT   C. ☐DOC   D.☐ TEXT

67.) Which of the following option is not available on Insert tab, Table

A. ☐Draw Table   B. ☐Convert text to Table
C. ☐Excel Spreadsheet   D. ☐Word Art

68.) To insert Drop Cap in one of the paragraphs you should access

A. ☐Home tab   B. ☐Insert tab
C. ☐References tab   D. ☐View tab

69. How many different positions can you set for Drop Cap?

A. ☐1   B. ☐2   C. ☐4   D.☐ 6

70. Which of the following can **NOT** be used to create parallel style columns?

A. ☐Page layout tab   B. ☐Insert Table
B. ☐Insert Textbox   D. ☐Home tab Columns

71.) Which of the following is used to create newspaper style columns?

A. ☐Format tab   B. ☐Insert Table
C. ☐Insert Textbox   D. ☐Page layout, Columns

72.) Columns dialog box can be opened from...................................

A. ☐Page Layout tab, columns, more columns
B. ☐Double click on column space in ruler
C. ☐Press Alt + O + C
D. ☐All of above

73.) You can jump to the next column containing text by...................

A. ☐Clicking with your mouse on the next column
B. ☐Press Alt + down arrow
C. ☐both of above
D. ☐None of above

74.) How can you break the current column and start a new column immediately?

A. ☐Press Ctrl + Shift + Enter B. ☐Press Alt + Enter
C. ☐Press Ctrl + Enter   D. ☐Press Alt + Shift + Enter

75.) If the number of columns selected is 2 and the line between check box is activated, where is the line drawn?
- A. ☐in the left margin
- B. ☐in the right margin
- C. ☐both in the left and right margin
- D. ☐in the middle of the columns

76.) To open Columns dialog box quickly
- A. ☐double click on the left margin area of ruler
- B. ☐double the space between area on ruler
- C. ☐double click the right margin in ruler
- D. ☐All of above

77.) Which of the following commands is not available on View tab?
- A.☐Zoom
- B. ☐Thumbnails
- C. ☐Gridlines
- D. ☐Track changes

78.) Text boundaries can be displayed or hidden from..........................
- A. ☐ Auto text option from Insert tab
- B. ☐File Tab, Options, Advanced
- C. ☐Customize from Word Options
- D. ☐All of the above

79.) Which of the following are Word Processing Programs?
- A. ☐Microsoft Word
- B. ☐Word Perfect
- C. ☐Microsoft Word Pad
- D.) ☐All of above

80.) Microsoft Office provides help in many ways, which of these is one of them?
- A. ☐What is this?
- B. ☐Office Assistant
- C. ☐Help menu
- D. ☐All of above

81.) There can be many ways to insert page numbers in a document. Which of the following lets you insert page numbers.
- A. ☐Page Number from Insert tab
- B. ☐Page Set up from Page layout tab
- C. ☐Insert Footnote from References tab
- D. ☐Both A and C

82.) Which of the following is not the part of Standard Office Suite?
- A. ☐Word Processor
- B. ☐Database
- C. ☐Image Editor
- D. ☐File manager

83.) Where can you find the draw Table command?

A. ☐Page Layout tab, Table   B. ☐Home Tab, Table

C. ☐Mailings Tab, Table   D. ☐Insert Tab, Table

84.) Which of the following option on File tab pull down menu is used to close Microsoft Word document?

A. ☐Quit   B. ☐Close   C. ☐Exit   D. ☐New

85.) Superscript, subscript, outline, emboss, engrave are known as.....

A. ☐font styles   B. ☐font effects

C. ☐word art   D. ☐text effects

86.) Shimmer, Sparkle text, blinking background etc known as text animation found only in Microsoft Word 2003 and known as...............

A. ☐font styles   B. ☐font effects

C. ☐word art   D. ☐text effects

87.) The feature of Microsoft Word that automatically adjusts the amount of space between certain combinations of characters so that an entire word looks more evenly spaced. What is that feature called?

A. ☐Spacing   B. ☐Scaling

C. ☐Kerning   D. ☐Positioning

88.) Which of the following is not available in Font Spacing?

A. ☐Normal   B. ☐Loosely

C. ☐Condensed   D. ☐Expanded

89.)Which of the following position is not available for fonts on Microsoft Word?

A. ☐Normal   B. ☐Raised

C. ☐Lowered   D. ☐Centered

90.) Bold, Italic, Regular are known as...

A. ☐font styles   B. ☐font effects

C. ☐word art   D. ☐text effects

91.) If you need to hide some paragraphs, how can you do it?

A. ☐From paragraph dialog box   B. ☐From Font dialog box

C. ☐From Options dialog box   D. ☐None of above

92. Which of the following is the latest version of Microsoft Word?

A. ☐Microsoft Word 2007   B. ☐Microsoft Word 2010

C. ☐Microsoft Word 2013   D. ☐Microsoft Word 2014

93.) Changing the appearance of a document is called?

A. ☐Proofing   B. ☐Editing

C. ☐Formatting   D. ☐All of above

94.) You can detect spelling and grammar errors by...........................

    A. ☐Press Shift + F7   B. ☐Press Ctrl + F7

    C. ☐Press Alt + F7   D. ☐Press F7

95.) A program installed to type mathematical text in Microsoft Word 2003 and older verisons of Microsoft Word is called?

    A. ☐Equation program   B. ☐Math Type

    C. ☐Equation Type   D. ☐Symbols Type

96.) The Page range **All** on the Print dialog box will print.....................

    A. ☐the page containing the insertion point

    B. ☐every page in the document

    C. ☐the text you have selected

    D. ☐pages you specify

97.) The simplest way to create text that is lined up in columns without inserted columns before typing is to.................................

    A. ☐use Tabs Stops   B. ☐use Space bar

    C. ☐use table with no borders   D. ☐All of above

98.) To assign a password for your document you.............................

    A. ☐Click on File tab, Save As, Tools, General Options

    B. ☐Click on Insert tab, Insert password

    C. ☐Click on File, Options, Proofing

    D. ☐Click on File tab, Word Options, Save, General Options

99.) To add page borders

    A. ☐Click on Insert tab, borders and shading

    B. ☐Click Page layout tab, Page Borders, Bordrers and Shading, Page borders, Art drop down list

    C. ☐Click on Insert tab, Picture, Insert

    D. ☐Click on Insert tab, Clip Art

100.) To Redo your last action press ....A. ☐Ctrl + Y

    B. ☐Ctrl + P   C. ☐Ctrl + R   C. ☐Alt + R

Internet

1. What is the Internet?..

....

....(2mks)

2. Give five (5) advantages of electronic mail.....................................

....

....

....

....

....

....(10mks)

3. Name four search engines used on the World Wide Web.................

....

....

....(2mks)

4. Name four web browsers of your choice.......................................

....

....

....

....(4mks)

5. What is e-Learning?...

....

....

....

....(2mks)

5. What is e-Commerce?...

....

....

....(2mks)

6. What are the five main elements of e-Commerce?.........................

....

....

....

....

....

....

....

....

....

....

....

....
....
....
....
....
....
....
....
....
....(10mks)

7. What do you understand by surfing?..
....
....(1mk)

8. Write in full the following:
(i) http:..
....
....(2mks)

(ii) www..
....
....(2mks)

(iii)URL:...
....
....(2mks)

Wifi..
....(2mks)

9. What is Facebook?..
....
....(2mks)

10. Describe how you would create an email account with any online
    service?..
....
....
....
....
....
....

....

....

....

....

....

....

....

....

....

....

....

....

....

....

....

....

....

....

....

....

....

....

....

....

....

....(10mks)

11. Describe how you would sign in with Facebook and explain how you can place your face picture on facebook timeline

....

....

....

....

....

....

....
....
....
....
....
....
....
....
....
....
....(10mks)

b.) How would you share a picture on a friend's wall on facebook?...

....
....
....(2mks)

c.) Name five other popular social media sites you know.....................

....
....
....
....
....
....
....
....(5mks)

Multiple Choice Questions (MCQs)

Tick (√) the correct answer

1....................is a file in a format the computer can directly execute.

☐Executable file   ☐Read only file   ☐Hidden file

2. Accessing files on one computer from a different computer is known as...........................

☐Emailing   ☐Chatting   ☐File sharing

3................... is a hardware or software that secures computer files by blocking unauthorized access.

☐Malware ☐Firewall ☐Spyware

4. Someone who breaks into your computer over the Internet is known as...................

☐Spy ☐Hacker ☐Scammer

5. A feature offered by many online services that allow participants to converse by typing messages which are displayed almost instantly is called.................................

☐Chat ☐Net meeting ☐Yahoo messenger

6...................is an E-mail-based discussion forum dedicated to a topic of interest.

☐Mailing list ☐Net meeting ☐Yahoo messenger

7. A hardware device that allows computers to communicate with each other by transmitting signals over telephone lines is called ....

☐Modem ☐USB ☐iPOD

8. The name given to a web site where people can converse with each other by typing messages which are displayed almost instantly on the screens of others on the online forum is ....

☐chat room ☐discussion forum ☐online messaging

9. ....is an online electronic bulletin board, where users can read and post comments about a specific topic.

☐Discussion group ☐Facebook ☐Netlog

10. Copying files from one computer to another and can also mean viewing a web site, or material on a Web server, with a Web browser is known as................................

☐Downloading ☐Browsing ☐Surfing

11. The first page on a Web site, which introduces the site and provides the means of navigation, is called.............................

☐Google ☐Homepage ☐Navigation page

12. A set of four numbers, each between zero and 255, separated by periods (e.g. 192.168.0.5) is known ....

☐IP number ☐Password ☐ISP number

13............................... is the name of web sites designed for children under 13 years old, or which attract visitors who are under 13 years old.

☐Pupils' web sites ☐Under 13 web sites ☐Kids' web sites

14.......................is the coded format language used for creating hypertext documents on the World Wide Web and controlling how Web pages appear.

☐HTML   ☐HTTP   ☐TCP/IP

15. The standard language that computers connected to the World Wide Web use to communicate with each other is..............................

☐HTML   ☐HTTP   ☐TCP/IP

16. A portion of text on a Web page that is linked to another Web page is called?.................

☐Hyperlink   ☐Coloured text   ☐Button

17. A private network inside a company or organization, which uses software like that used on the Internet, but is for internal use only, and is not accessible to the public is called.................................

☐Intranet   ☐Local Network   ☐Dial up

18. Information presented in more than one format, such as text, audio, video, graphics, and images are called............

☐Data   ☐Multimedia   ☐Poly information

19...............................is the informal rules of Internet courtesy, enforced exclusively by other Internet users.

☐Etiquette   ☐Courtesy   ☐Netiquette

20.Discussion groups on the Internet are called?..............................

☐Newsgroups   ☐Chatters   ☐Chat groups

21.The main program that runs on a computer is called......................

☐Operating System   ☐Microsoft   ☐Window

22. An identity theft scam in which criminals send out spam that imitates the look and language of legitimate correspondence from e-commerce sites.

☐Scammers   ☐Phishing   ☐Scams

23. Sending a message to a discussion group or other public message area on the Internet is called..

☐Emailing   ☐Attaching   ☐Posting

24. Digital entities such as bulletin boards, public directories where personal user data may be distributed by a site or a service provider are called...

☐Public forums   ☐Cyber Cafés   ☐Cyber Space

25...................is a tool that enables users to locate information on the World Wide Web.

☐Explorer ☐Search engine ☐Navigator

26. Unsolicited "junk" e-mail sent to large numbers of people to promote products or services is called......................................

☐Spam ☐Junk ☐Scam

27.......................... is the information that you provide to an online service provider when you sign up to become a member.

☐Subscription data ☐Sign in ☐Sign up

28. The process of removing a program from a computer is called.........

☐Delete ☐Remove ☐Uninstall

29. ....is an email address that is hard for spammers to guess, but easy for you to remember.

☐Unique email address ☐crtv@camnet.cm ☐unique@camnet.cm

30. A malicious program that is loaded onto your computer unknown to you and quickly using up all available memory is called..

☐Antivirus ☐Virus ☐Malicious

31. A collection of "pages" or files linked together and available on the World Wide Web is called........................

☐Web site ☐Internet ☐WWW

32. The person responsible for administering a Web site is called.........

☐Network administrator ☐Webmaster ☐IT Engineer

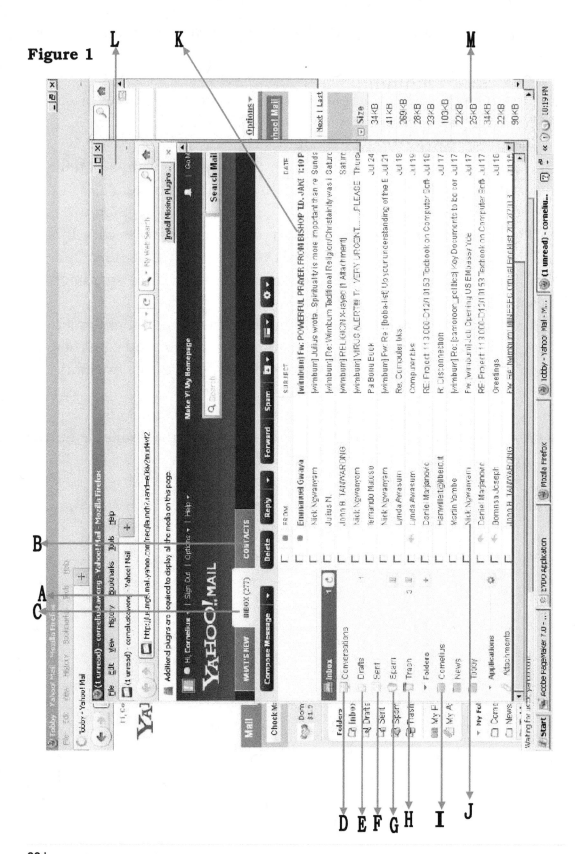

Figure 1

Figure 1 above shows an opened mail box in which emails is stored with Yahoo mail. The special purpose folders that come with Yahoo mail account are labeled B–H. Copy the names and give the functions of the parts labeled B–H.

Name:(A).............................Function...
....

Name:(B).............................Function...
....

Name:(C).............................Function...
....

Name:(D).............................Function...
....

Name:(E).............................Function...
....

Name:(F).............................Function...
....

Name:(G).............................Function...
....

Name:(H).............................Function...
....

Name:(A).............................Function...
....

1.) The part labeled I is a folder in the opened box created by owner. Sign in to your own email box and create a folder bearing your name so you can move incoming mails which you do not want stored in the inbox to this folder. Write the steps you have used on The Students Practice Workbook below...
....
....
....
....
....
....
....
....
....

....
....
....
....
....
....
....
....
....(10mks)

2.) Explain the part labeled **J**...
....
....
....
....
....
....
....(5mks)

3.) Explain the part labeled **K**...
....
....
....
....
....
....
....
....(5mks)

4.) Give the name and function of the part labeled **L**
Name:...
Function...
....
....
....
....
....(6mks)

5.) What does the part labeled **M** signifies?...

....

....

....

....

....

....

....

....

....(5mks)

....

....

....

....

....

....

....

....

....

....

....

....

....

....

....

....

....

....

....

....

....

....

....

www.ingramcontent.com/pod-product-compliance
Lightning Source LLC
La Vergne TN
LVHW080102070326
832902LV00014B/2369